THE SEARCH FOR
AMERICA'S FAITH

The
SEARCH for

George
GALLUP, Jr.

AMERICA'S FAITH

David POLING

Abingdon ★ Nashville

THE SEARCH FOR AMERICA'S FAITH

Library of Congress Cataloging in Publication Data

GALLUP, GEORGE. 1930–
    The search for America's faith.
    1. United States—Religion—1960– I. Poling, David, 1928– joint
author. II. Title.
BL2530.U6G34   209'.73   80-12619

ISBN 0-687-37090-6

Scripture quotations unless otherwise noted are from the Revised Standard
Version of the Bible, copyrighted 1946, 1952, © 1971, 1973 by the Division of
Christian Education of the National Council of the Churches of Christ in the
U.S.A.

MANUFACTURED BY THE PARTHENON PRESS AT
NASHVILLE, TENNESSEE, UNITED STATES OF AMERICA

Contents

Foreword

The reader of this book, like American society in general, is fascinated by the future. We are all interested, at times intoxicated, with what the trends, polls, and prophets say about the future of our lives. Surely it is not new for humankind to have a fascination with events yet to unfold. Prophecy is as old as scripture. Forecasting is as common as the satellite weather map on TV. Predictions concerning economic cycles, gold prices, and housing starts saturate our daily press. The communications network, now celestial as well as global, delivers every sort of glimpse possible about what lies ahead.

Consider the following. Members of the World Food Council project that the hunger crisis is getting worse rather than better. The next decade will require a $57 billion investment if the developing countries are to achieve just a 4 percent annual increase in food production. (Presently Canada and the United States produce more than half of the world's grain.)

The long-range weather forecast is staggeringly chilly—a computer specialist took snowfall figures for the past forty years and flatly states that the beginning of the 80s will mean massive amounts of snow for the Eastern cities. Pennie Du Pont, writing from Chicago, notes that Detroit, Pittsburgh, Boston, New York, Cleveland, and Erie, Pennsylvania, will far exceed the forty-year average in annual snowfall.

Here is the current copy of *Foreign Affairs,* the quarterly publication of the Council on Foreign Relations. The nine major articles deal with everything from code-breaking to boat people, essays on Nicaragua and Turkey, long studies of inflation and arms control. Every one of these articles deals with future expectations, good and bad. One suggests that the only way to solve the refugee horror story of southeast Asia is to reach a diplomatic accommodation with Hanoi; it speaks of "Brezhnev and Beyond," and it has a tormenting piece on the "Future of Soviet Jewry: Emigration or Assimilation." The future has us in its grip. What's happening today is already shaping the script of tomorrow, and this is terribly evident in the field of religious studies, attitudes, and beliefs. This volume seeks to draw some logical conclusions using the input of ideas and attitudes gathered from all over America.

Periodically, the religious intensity of our time approaches frenzy. The public gasps at the horror of Jonestown in Guyana or the absurd tactics of a Moslem fundamentalism reflected in the rule of Ayatollah

Khomeini and regrets all notions of religious allegiance. That extremes are flourishing in the realm of the spirit is evident, and certain contemporary writers have pronounced severe judgment upon the main-line churches, sensing their failure to meet the challenges of the latter part of the twentieth century. Said one editorial in the *Wall Street Journal,*

> Old beliefs have decayed and new beliefs have not sprung forward to replace them. The decay of religion is unmistakable. The appeal of the cults expresses the profoundness of the human will to believe, the longing for certainty of faith . . . the last place anyone would look today to fill this longing is any of the mainstream religious denominations. They have little time for faith, being preoccupied with such issues as how to govern South Africa. Even the Roman Catholic Church, with its millenniums of experience in sorting evil and good in the religious impulse, is losing its power to touch the soul. (November 30, 1978)

These concerns deserve thoughtful response. We need to know if our immediate apprehensions and anxieties with the present state of organized religion are a prelude to spiritual disaster or the final darkness before the dawn of a sparkling new day. Certain verifiable indicators tell us that hopeful trends are already in motion, such as the first upturn in church attendance in the United States in more than twenty years. And in spite of the preceding editorial about the Roman Catholic Church "losing its power to touch the soul," we are prepared now to debate that conclusion in the face of a significant surge within the

Catholic community, especially among youth and young marrieds.

While there is no doubt that the cults have attracted thousands of young people in North America, leading many into a weird, even destructive religious development, other signs are pointing to powerful recoveries in the main-line churches in the same age groups. Consider seminary enrollment. In the five-year span of 1973–1978, the Association of Theological Schools in the U.S. and Canada report an enrollment gain from 34,082 to 46,460. However, in almost the same breath, it must be conceded that the twenty-year decline in Catholic Sisters, from 98,000 in 1960 to less than 46,000 as of this writing, is a sharp blow to the teaching vocation of that religious community. (The number of sisters representing all orders employed in hospital and social work, as well as teaching professions, had a twenty-year decline, dropping from 164,576 to the current 129,391.)

It would be difficult to identify a decade that incorporated more crises and change for the churches than the 1970s. Yet the 1980s may far surpass the tumultuous furor we have just completed. Staggering membership losses suffered by the main-line denominations have not yet turned around in a positive growth direction. The Presbyterian, Episcopalian, and United Church of Christ communions cannot long exist as viable church organizations nationally if the declines of the 70s persist in the 1980s.

On the other hand, the conservative churches appear to be in an up period, with the Southern Baptists and a variety of fundamentalist groups setting attendance and membership records almost hourly. Among para-Christian bodies, perhaps most impressive is the steady advance of the Mormon Church as it makes theological corrections within its dogma, e.g., the acceptance of blacks into its priesthood. Incidentally, readers will find in the pages ahead revealing illustrations of how the different religious groups view each other—some are terribly antagonistic toward each other, nearly at the rock-throwing stage, while others demonstrate surprising respect and admiration for their spiritual neighbors—which may be a prelude to new adventures in cooperation, and even merger.

Two other trends are clear and provocative: Confidence in the church and organized religion remains very strong compared to nine other key institutions in American life; and most Americans continue to place a great deal of importance on their religious beliefs. How these sentiments affect the religious climate of the United States is a theme that we will now pursue together.

George Gallup, Jr.
David Poling

The Yearnings of Youth

Young people in America are vitally concerned about their religious faith. Some of this concern translates into sharp, persistent criticism of the institutional church for its failure to match up to its message. Yet teenagers and young adults reveal how they can be reached, and new avenues are proposed for their involvement. How and why cults flourish, with notes on the response of the church to this spiritual challenge, are also the subjects of this chapter.

Youth and the Church

As America was deeply and permanently shaped by the youthful protests of the 1960s, so the religious community of the 1980s will be designed and fashioned from the many proposals now being suggested by this country's 25 million teenagers. Studies and recent surveys continue to underline the yearning, attention, and enthusiasm that young people are putting into their religious pursuits. Teenagers reveal an abiding interest in spiritual questions and high levels of personal involvement. One of our surveys found that nearly nine out of ten teenagers pray, an extraordinarily high proportion believe in God (or a universal spirit), and only one out of a hundred says that he or she *does not* have some kind of religious preference or affiliation.

At the same time, this group indicates distance from organized religion, frustration over the church's role in society, and a generally negative attitude toward churchgoers and church members. Their heavenly hopes are far from fulfilled in the earthbound churches. Only one-fourth admitted a "high degree" of confidence in organized religion compared to 38 percent of the adult population, which gave a strong endorsement to the official religious community in America. What these young people regret most is the failure of the church to reach out to the people they *should* be serving. They perceive that the practices of the church do not square with the teachings of Christ.

Young people, teenagers, claim a deep relationship to God; indeed, a higher proportion of those polled believe in a personal God than do their parents. Four in ten say that religion plays a very important role in their lives (with the tally increasing to five in ten among older teenage girls). They are disappointed that the churches do not have many youth programs. This is not a new complaint. A decade ago a major study covering the religious attitudes and practices of Presbyterian teenagers revealed that 44 percent of those active in congregational life went *outside* of church programs to find fellowship in such associations as Youth for Christ, Young Life, and King's Teens.

The flourishing of religious movements and cults outside the mainstream of the established churches and their appeal for today's teenagers and young people further attest to the problem. The weakening of traditional values has caught up with the emerging generation and if the church does not respond, young people will find an agency, movement, or experience that does. Current studies indicate that six unorthodox religious movements have attracted enough attention in the United States to merit examination. They are Transcendental Meditation (T.M.), yoga, the charismatic movement, mysticism, faith healing, and various Eastern religions. More than twenty-seven million people have been in touch—superficially or deeply— with these religious expressions. For young people under 30, involvement in and exploration of such religious adventures far exceeds the overall national experience. The attention given by young adults is nearly double that given by older adults to yoga, T.M., and the Eastern religions. Clearly the deep spiritual hunger of young people is not being met by the established church.

Many young people seem quite comfortable with a solitary, personal approach to matters of faith—so much so that three out of four state that they believe a person can be a good Christian even if he or she does *not* attend church. Should that attitude prevail for long, it means an absolute goodbye to the present religious arrangement in North America. But before we hang a bolt of crepe and proceed with the last rites, let us consider some specific complaints of youth toward the church as well as some of the positive signals they are sending.

The negative attitude of young people toward organized religion generally issues in the following complaints: the failure of churches genuinely to serve those whom Christ loved and sought and reclaimed; the shallow and superficial stance of so many church members; the inability of congregations to deal with the basics of faith and appeal to youth on a solid spiritual basis; the absence of the feeling of excitement or warmth within the church's fellowship; negative feelings about the clergy in charge. Regarding the latter, four in ten young adults state that honesty and the personal ethical standards of clergy are "only average," "low," or "very low." This startling conclusion calls for in-depth exploration. It may be true, however, that the negative attitudes of youth toward churchgoers and the institutional church are a result of distance from and ignorance about congregational life. Young people are often critical of the church because they see it linked to other social institutions in American society that appear to be unconcerned or ineffective when dealing with primary human problems. Congress, the military, big business, and big labor receive even sharper barbs from the youthful commentators in our surveys.

The findings of the 1976 Dayton Study revealed that 44 percent considered unemployment and the high cost of living to be the most important problems facing the country today.[1] To a large extent, especially for minority youth, those problems have intensified. "Lack of leadership" in the nation and "political corruption" were alarming to 35 percent of those polled. Lack of trust and communication, crime and lawlessness, absence of religion and morality, followed in that order.

Although disillusioned by the institutions of North American society, the young adults in the Dayton Study still cling to the traditional values and standards that many would consider the norm. For the majority of women interviewed, the ideal life was to be married and have children. While very liberal in their attitudes toward premarital sex and the use of birth control methods, three-fourths of those interviewed did not think that abortion should be legal under all circumstances. The majority see no moral question at stake in homosexuality as a life-style, but four in ten believe it is wrong and so condemn it.

In spite of their generally low opinion of American institutions, the young people in this Ohio study indicate strong attraction for volunteer work and a high consideration for social work as a career option. Their humanitarian impulse appears to be fueled by their valuing a Christian orientation which they believe the church to have neglected or given a rather low priority. Some 40 percent believed that the church was failing to

---

[1]The Dayton Study—"Attitudes, Values and Lifestyles of Young Adults in Greater Dayton." Copyright, 1976 by Miami Valley Young Adult Ministry, Inc. Study conducted by The Gallup Organization, Inc., 53 Bank St., Princeton, N.J. 08540.

do its proper job in society through its neglect of the poor and underprivileged, its spiritual apathy, its excessive materialism, its hypocritical stance, its out-of-date approach to youth, and its avoidance of moral problems. John McKay would say, "Let the Church be the Church," and this generation would add, "Right on."

Young people were blunt when responding to the in-depth Dayton survey: "The Church is worried about the condition of the world and not worried about its own people; it tries to save the world while people in the Church go to hell," said a young Presbyterian. A member from the United Church of Christ remarked, "They are too worried about building finer churches and not worried enough about doing what the Church was set up for."

Superficial Christianity was alarming to many young people. The Sunday-only attitude seemed fruitless, frustrating, and dishonest to the Lordship of Christ. Observed one young Methodist: "Churches should try to reach those who don't come into their buildings, and help those who don't believe, try to see how God can work through simple ways such as feeding a hungry family or painting someone's house."

While the persons queried were asking for more relevance in daily life, they resented the failure of the churches to deepen their perception of God and to widen their experience in spiritual pursuits. Said one individual who had been raised a Presbyterian but now considered himself without a religious preference, "They spend too much time preaching birth control, abortion, and such and do nothing to help those who need understanding and counseling."

While the activism of the churches had its share of critics, the youth in the Dayton survey were overwhelming in their judgment that the church should give *equal* consideration to the personal needs of the individual believer and the social problems of the wider society. When asked if the churches should refrain from social and political matters, 52 percent replied that the churches should express their views and make known their position to the public.

Asked whether religious beliefs affected their own actions, 26 percent said their religious beliefs affected their daily thinking and ethics, and another 39 percent suggested that they had some effect on their daily behavior. Only 12 percent said their beliefs had "no effect" whatever. This generation is seeking to translate faith into fulfillment, and to bring religion into the harsh realities of the hour. Religion is on their mind: 62 percent said that during a twenty-four hour period God and religion had been on their mind, 20 percent saying it was through prayer, 19 percent through church or family devotions. Looking to the future, the Dayton group predicted that their religious convictions would be *very* important to them ten years from now. In fact, 75 percent of those who responded noted that religious beliefs would be fairly or very important in their lives. Of that group, 64 percent had Sunday school training; another 21 percent, training in parochial school; and some 20 percent, instruction in religious matters by their parents.

A measure of church attendance among these young

people found 26 percent in church Sunday-by-Sunday
and 74 percent not regularly in the pews. Since 1976
when this poll was taken, the attendance among the
young adult group has significantly increased, nationally, by more than 10 percent. It may be that much of
the disillusionment and disarray of the 60s and early 70s
has at last given way to a more generous view of the
institutional church and a deeper participation in its
programs.

Nationally, young people continue to prod the
church into fresh and decisive action—both to improve
the church and to enrich the quality of our national life.
Racial injustice, segregation, and the oppression of
minorities continue to capture the attention of young
adults. A recent Gallup poll showed that while most
whites worship in a segregated church (in fact 46
percent report that there are no blacks in attendance in
their congregation), a majority of whites state that they
would *welcome* blacks to their services. When white
young people replied to the same question, over 70
percent said they would welcome blacks to their church
and would like to see them participating. It is
interesting to note that in all age groups, Catholics
reported the highest percentage of blacks in attendance
(60 percent) and also extended the highest welcome for
more to be there next week (72 percent).

The West is leading America in the positive
response to integration in the church. Some 67
percent of those attending church in the West (blacks
and whites) claim that blacks are in regular attendance, and a high of 83 percent would like to see this
increase. Again, white young people are leading the

surge with the college-educated generation most eager to have a much wider participation of blacks in all levels of congregational life. Young people are already shaping the future through their criticism of the faults of the faithful and their positive, aggressive stance for meaningful improvement in human relationships.

This forward-looking trend is also seen in the attitudes of young adults toward the ordination of women. While the majority of main-line churches endorse female clergy, the conservative wings of Judaism, Lutheranism, and Eastern Orthodoxy remain in opposition. The largest Christian body to resist this change is the Roman Catholic Church. Pope Paul VI issued a declaration in 1977 denying women ordination to the priesthood—a decree supported by the majority of Catholics in the U.S. Fifty-seven percent of the national Catholic population voiced their disagreement with the proposal that women be ordained. The response was nearly reversed, however, when those under 30 were sampled. Fifty-four percent stated they would favor the ordination of women to the office of priesthood. Again, college-educated single people living in the West were strongest in their support of this change. The youthful Protestant counterparts—those under 30—were overwhelmingly in favor of women's ordination. Those in the 18–24 age group had the highest percentage in favor—54 percent—of any group save the Presbyterians, who favored women's ordination by 56 percent.

We have heard that young people today are an inward, self-centered generation, who say "do your

own thing" and who have disdainfully removed
themselves from the strain and severity of modern life.
Our studies reveal the opposite: many are vitally
interested in the helping professions and one out of
every four people 14 years of age or older volunteer
time to some nonprofit organization. The youth in
Dayton, studied in the Gallup-directed survey of 735
individuals, with all their *angst* over unresponsive
American institutions, like the suggestion that a law be
enacted requiring some form of service to the nation in
the year following high school. Forty percent of the
young people said they would favor such service if it
included not only the armed forces but also tours of
alternate duty in conservation, VISTA, hospital work,
and the Peace Corps. An even higher percent of this
group indicated that they would consider donating
some of their time to church activities on a regular basis
if they were asked. Nearly half said they would respond
to requests for their help in Sunday school, Christian
education, youth activities, as well as in a wide variety
of tasks in social work, church music, sports programs,
and fellowship events.

Recent Gallup polls have shown that teenagers
attend church with a regularity that is as high, if not
higher, than older persons. Seventy-one percent of
teenagers say they are church members; and as we have
said before, only 1 percent indicate no religious
preference or affiliation. The appeal of religious
retreats and spiritual growth weekends is significant
with this age group—46 percent of the boys and 57
percent of the girls said they would respond positively
to invitations to such events. A projected 5 percent of

the boys and girls in America expressed a specific interest in a religious vocation.

The Cults

The intensive survey of the greater Dayton community of young people revealed that 31 percent of those polled had been involved with a variety of religious movements and cults, ranging from faith healing, the charismatic movement, and Eastern religions to astrology, yoga, and T.M. (The Unification Church of Rev. Moon had not yet arrived on these shores in early 1972.) Thirty-one percent, one in three, is a rather high involvement for a group of which 75 percent state they believe Jesus Christ is the Son of God. The same group of young men and women also believed in the truth of the resurrection of Christ by a strong 75 percent, with nearly 70 percent seeing the Bible as the Word of God or at least partially so. Nevertheless, Christian churches are losing their youth, at least temporarily, by the thousands to other religions or cults. The Christian churches of America, liberal, conservative, evangelical, and fundamental, must now perceive a common enemy in the cults or expect serious decline in their current membership and their future prospects.

The latest arrival on the religious landscape of America, the Unification Church, has met with the greatest resistance and negative reaction of any group discussed. Initially, Rev. Moon appeared in the United States at the head of a massive Honor America campaign, proclaiming that God did not want Richard Nixon kicked out of the White House. His program reached major cities from coast to coast, and the Unification Church began to swell with new recruits, nicely dressed, well-behaved, and terribly earnest about the Moon doctrine.

Moon's early-on success with mass rallies, using beguiling choruses of small children and great bushels of beautiful flowers, was soon met with the suspicion and later hostility of the Christian community. The Baptists were particularly incensed with the Moon notion that John the Baptist was a failure—for if his program had succeeded, the world would, according to the Korean guru, have been prepared for Christ and not ended up crucifying him. It seems that in Moon's heresy, Jesus as well as his cousin, John, was also a dramatic failure.

Among the revelations espoused by Moon, a deposed Presbyterian minister from Korea, was the thought that it was God's original plan that Adam and Eve marry and that their children be perfect and sinless. Alas, Satan intervened and is the real master of the world. Moon preaches that now the world is in the last days, that a new Messiah is soon to come—or in fact, may already be on earth patiently waiting to be recognized. Further revelations developed by Moon state that this new Messianic figure is definitely a man born in Korea in this century. He will become, in time, the father of a Perfect Family (which Adam and Eve failed to create) who will redeem humankind and begin the promised millennium, when wars will cease, sickness and sin will vanish, the hungry and sorrowful will be filled according to their need, and the whole world will join to celebrate universal peace.

Moon's followers are expected to surrender all their wealth and worldly possessions, retaining just a minimum to get by on; they find employment only to assist the movement through their wages and salaries. While the followers adopt a frugal life-style, Moon-watchers have noticed his attraction to large estates, great tax-free land holdings in New York City and Westchester County, plus a bountiful conglomerate of factories and munitions works in Korea.

The most positive response to Rev. Moon comes from the younger age groups, particularly those under 30, single, and living in the West. The followers of Moon are sincere and committed. Said one believer:

> Moon's movement is a reflection of the dissatisfaction of American youth with society and their need for something in which to believe. It's not hard for me to see why some young people are attracted to Moon.

Said another:

> In my view, the Moonies have been victimized by a media campaign against them—sort of a witchhunt. I don't think they're guilty of all they have been accused of.

National ratings are one way by which the broader Christian community can sample the impact of prominent, even global, personalities in religion and sort out the perceptions the public has about these leaders' beliefs and practices. In 1977 the Gallup Poll invited a cross section of Americans to express their attitudes toward Billy Graham, Pope Paul VI, and Rev. Sun Myung Moon. Despite accusations of financial machinations, America's most visible Protestant, the Rev. Billy Graham, maintains a very favorable image in the eyes of the public. In 1977, Pope Paul VI was the world's best-known Catholic, and he enjoyed a positive image with Americans— one that was improving during his last year in the Vatican. The most famous practitioner of alternative religion in the United States, the Rev. Sun Myung Moon, elicited one of the most overwhelmingly negative responses ever reported by a major national poll.

Using a ten-point scale which ranged from extremely favorable to extremely unfavorable, Graham gained 41 percent extremely favorable and 5 percent very negative; Pope Paul garnered 37 percent extremely favorable and 3 percent the other extreme; and the Korean evangelist collected 1 percent extremely favorable and 51 percent extremely unfavorable. In the more than twenty years the Gallup Poll has been asking Americans to rate various people, only Nikita Khrushchev and Fidel Castro have received more negative ratings than currently accorded Rev. Moon.

No single group gives Moon more than a 3 percent highly favorable rating, the highest overall favorable reactions coming from those under 30 years old and from non-whites—both give him a 10 percent favorable rating. Thus, in the ocean of negative readings only the idealistic, the inquisitive, and those turned-off to the establishment and institutional religion have any good points for the Korean cleric.[2]

The greatest animosity toward Moon comes from college-educated, upper-income, white-collar professionals in North America. Catholics and Protestants are equally hostile in their reaction to Moon, with Protestants being slightly more intense in their feelings, and Episcopalians being the most intense with 75 percent rejecting the Far Eastern pilgrim.

In an Associated Press Gallup Youth Survey covering the Unification Church, one 17-year-old high school student seemed to represent many of his peers when he said, "I have always had my doubts about any organization in which the individual loses his identity, and it appears that this group is very capable of establishing a 'group identity.' "

The Crime of the Cults

While unfavorable opinions abound concerning various cults and the Moon group in particular, at the same time there are many in America who say they are either not familiar with the movement—as high as 59 percent polled—or else choose to reserve judgment—some 8 percent. But the excitement, adventure, intrigue, commotion, and tragedies associated with the cults in recent years have increased awareness of the presence of the cults and the dangers that many of them create for young and old.

------

[2]"Religion in America," The Gallup Opinion Index, Report No. 145, 1977–1978, pp. 104-5.

The mass suicides and murders in Jonestown, Guyana, were the most widely followed events in 1978, with a remarkable 98 percent of the American public saying that they had heard about this tragic occurrence in Latin America. In fact, few events in the entire forty-three-year history of the Gallup Poll have been known and discussed by such a high proportion of the U.S. population. Even among those persons with only a grade-school education, as many as 96 percent said they had heard or read about the deaths in Guyana among the members of the People's Temple cult led by Rev. Jim Jones.

When the public was asking in the aftermath of November 18, 1978, "How could this have happened?" and "Could it happen again?" the Gallup Poll asked Americans in all walks of life to provide the reasons for which people might become implicated with cults of this kind. Generally respondents said, "The need for leadership and a father figure" or "Unhappy lives and a feeling of hopelessness." Many mentioned the need that countless people have for a deeper meaning to life and the failure of the nation's churches to truly speak to the spiritual requirements of individuals.

There are steady themes running through all the responses to questions about cults in America. Their existence seems to indicate that young people want to positively enrich and develop their spiritual lives. Their expectation has been that this task belonged to the established churches of America. People are surprised, alarmed, and resentful that the churches are not taking seriously this God-given responsibility and instead wander off on secondary pursuits and superficial outings, and are unwilling to participate, sustain, and support those religious communities that live and teach a high noble calling and practice what they preach.

When we consider the rise and advance of cults in Western civilization, we should be aware of the multiple forces at work, e.g., the weakening of family life, the rapid rise in the divorce rate, the mobility and unpredictability of daily life, and the cumulative surge of rapid social change. Young people who are free from the normal restraint of family, the coercive pressures of relatives and neighbors—the monitoring of behavior that follows a person who is known by name and occupation become much more willing to experiment with drugs, to seek adventures in the illicit and occult, and to be prey for those organizations which offer instant friendship, immediate support, and prompt participation in remodeling the world.

Yet the joy of membership and belonging to cults often turn into a new regimentation as rigid and tedious, and much more threatening, than the faith once denied. In many groups, brainwashing techniques were rumored, and group manipulation seemed to be a daily happening. It was easy to join one of the cults, but at times it bordered on the dangerous to make a grand statement of resignation.

The new religions of the East with their exotic promise for the soul were to surge and then fade almost as fast as the gurus could charter jets or sign up public auditoriums for "love feasts." But the cults were something else, more sly and menacing, able to blend with the social fabric, their religious terrorists could strike and then disappear with hardly a trace save the tread from their late model van and a few empty flower cans across from the Gulf service station.

Martin Marty noted this when he concluded that

> not all the new groups were gentle. Some of the more
> durable ones were hardline cults. They were accused of
> luring young people from the family circle, subjecting
> them to various techniques of psychological manipula-
> tion, fencing them in with rules and regulations, and
> maybe even separating them with physical distance
> from the larger society.[3]

Without question, many people, especially the young, enter the cultic climate in search of release from drug enslavement or the inability to control their personal sexual behavior or to sustain meaning-ful relationships at home or with school friends. The initial deliverance may feel OK temporarily, but the new bondage about to be enforced is yet to be understood.

The cultic enterprise is so often faceless and submerged. While many young people quickly and easily spot and resist the enticements of Hare Krishna and the heavy-handed salesmanship of Rev. Moon, they are not prepared for the soft-spoken style of the Christian counterfeit groups which are now manifest in almost every major city. If the main-line churches are serious about the complaints and cries of youth, they will find themselves entering into a whole new

---

[3]Jackson W. Carroll, Douglas W. Johnson, and Martin E. Marty, *Religion in America: 1950 to the Present* (New York: Harper & Row, 1979), p. 82.

period of program, attention, and care of the young around them. Some suggestions for strategy and response are in order.

1. Each congregation should endeavor to have a special ministry or ministries to teenagers. Right now too many churches have virtually ignored this age group, concentrating instead on preteens and adults. The reason for this attitude is the feeling among many church leaders that they cannot successfully compete with all the other interests, loyalties, and time-commitments of youth. In the churches that can afford staff, too frequently that person is part-time or temporary, or at best, an inadequately trained layperson. By establishing a special youth ministry, a congregation embarks on an enterprise worthy of the community's priority. Often the prevailing notion has been that all churches have to do is wait until these young people grow up, get married, have a job, a mortgage, car payments, and children, and then they will be back in church looking for support and guidance. Wrong. There is no such guarantee, spoken or written, save that many, perhaps even a majority, will turn their youthful disenchantment into hostility and rejection as adults. A true ministry to teenagers will never wait for them to appear at the church door, rather it will reach out to this age group wherever they are to be found.

2. Spiritual nourishment is one of the highest goals that young people presently have in their formative lives. Ironic that they should be telling the churches that they have great spiritual needs and aspirations.

The young indicate that they want to go deep into the great places of God through prayer, Bible study, and personal discipline. Recreation, activities, and entertainment are way down on the urgency scale for this generation of God-seekers. Relevance is no longer the code word in the religious quest of youth. Get used to a new word: spirituality.

3. In Saul Bellow's engaging novel *Humboldt's Gift,* a talented writer gives his good friend, Charlie, a super outline for a winning script. Humboldt is actually on his last leg, and he wants his friend to have a better shot at stage success, so the gift. In his letter of presentation, Humboldt closes with this elegant farewell:

> You are lazy, disgraceful, tougher than you think but not yet a dead loss. In part you are humanly okay. We are supposed to do something for our kind. Don't get frenzied about money. Overcome your greed. Better luck with women. Last of all—remember: we are not natural beings but supernatural beings.
>
> Lovingly, Humboldt[4]

It is just possible that this letter applies to the church and the youth of today—it reminds us that "we are supposed to do something for our kind." The arriving generation is more than hinting, now almost screaming, to be used in some demanding cause. As many as half of our teenage boys say they favor a plan of national service to their country and

---

[4](New York: Viking Press, 1975), p. 347.

community, in either military or non-military duty. Churches should be planning to offer specific assignments and activities that provide a reasonable outlet for this religious zeal seeking fulfillment. New studies continue to reinforce the view that young people have a very powerful social consciousness. The occupational choices preferred by teenagers are weighted heavily toward the helping and serving professions—teaching, social work, medical and health services, and community advocacy programs.

4. The urge of young people to serve may be expressed both within the religious fellowship and beyond the church. While many caring young members will not enter the ministry as a full-time vocation, a significant number may wish to become paraclergy. This could be a new and dynamic office throughout the Christian community, perhaps similar to the office of deacon in the Catholic church today. Paraclerics could be given a certain amount of formal training and serve apprenticeships with local pastors. Recently a Methodist minister of a large urban congregation hired several college students in his church to do hospital and shut-in calling during their Christmas vacation. The impact upon the sick, the shut-in, and the disabled was astounding. Men and women and children were thrilled to have the loving attention of vital, concerned young men. Paraclergy could be used to manage a Help Line telephone ministry, organize transportation systems for the elderly or handicapped, pioneer fresh programs at prison and detention centers, create

social support events for singles who by the thousands are desperate for a fellowship alternative to the suffocating bar scene in America.

5. With the flurry and frenzy of the cults in North America and western Europe, sensitive main-line churches may discover that meaningful response will come only through three strategies:

   A. The recruitment of mature young men and women to study the cultic explosion and the Christian alternative to its leaders' audacious claims. A passive, hand-wringing reaction no longer suits the drama and danger of the hour.

   B. Congregations will now find it necessary to establish sophisticated gospel teams capable of presenting programs and events in order that youngsters on the edges of society, disconnected from the support of a strong family life and healthy institutional curriculum, have some clues to the perils now waiting the unsuspecting. Mental and spiritual health is as important to the wholeness of society as is pure water and clean air.

   C. With the rampant growth of the cultic enterprise, there are now thousands of young people and dislocated singles who have been practically—emotionally, spiritually, and psychologically—demolished by their downhill run with the so-called new religions. Just as the underground railroad was operated by religious communities such as the Quakers to assist runaway slaves in their dash to Canadian freedom, so today there is a dire need for half-way houses and hostels of renewal and recovery for those leaving the cults and escaping from the clutches of spiritual imprisonment. Through the centuries Christian orders gave shelter, safety, and sanctuary to the bruised souls of the Middle Ages. Again, the wider fellowship of concerned Christians can provide the places of recovery and rest for those broken by their own folly—or worse, by the betrayal of self-annointed messiahs and self-proclaimed gurus.

6. The pursuit of the inner life must take on a new urgency for the people of God. Strange, isn't it, that churches should be directed to rediscover the sanctuary within before they can reclaim the youth who have found them unfulfilling and vague about soul-seeking? Yet biblical history reminds us that organizations grow stale and appointed religious leaders become callous and self-serving. The appearance of young people in the Scriptures invaribly is a sign of the judgment of God and his intention that people, society, and the affairs of the Temple experience radical change. Younger saints are always given the dreadful assignment of letting the people in charge have the bad news: they are out of touch with God and their world is filled with disharmony, insensitivity, and injustice. Read again the call of young Samuel, young Isaiah, or young Jeremiah. Each has a profound reluctance to speak the heavy judgment of the Lord, but there it is, and the awareness and openness of youth was created to serve the purposes of God. In Jeremiah we read:

Now the word of the Lord came to me saying,
"Before I formed you in the womb I knew you,
and before you were born I consecrated you;
I appointed you a prophet to the nations." (1:4-5)

Jeremiah is young, but old enough to admit that this
is a wild, fierce assignment, one not to be taken
lightly and one, certainly, to be resented by those
people in charge of holy things, of running
kingdoms, or of collecting rents. So he replies,

"Ah, Lord God! Behold, I do not know how to speak,
    for I am only a youth." But the Lord said to me,
"Do not say, 'I am only a youth';
for to all to whom I send you you shall go,
and whatever I command you you shall speak.
Be not afraid of them,
for I am with you to deliver you, says the Lord."
                                                                    (1:6-8)

Then in terms reminiscent of Isaiah and his call,
Jeremiah describes the moment of his divine/human
encounter:

Then the Lord put forth his hand and touched my
    mouth; and the Lord said to me,
"Behold, I have put my words in your mouth.
See, I have set you this day over nations and over
    kingdoms,
to pluck up and to break down,
to destroy and to overthrow,
to build and to plant." (1:9-10)

In developing a significant and lasting youth ministry churches will want to be conscious of an inherent partnership, yes even encourage the style shown first in this vivid passage from Jeremiah. Only as churches recognize youth as meaningful, valid participants, not consumers or some sort of customer to be cultivated, but able and vigorous participants called by God, will we see the possibility of great change and advance for established institutions.

The New Testament church reveals a great expectancy, and even dependency, on the leadership role of young believers. Said Paul to Timothy:

> Train yourself in godliness; for while bodily training is of some value, godliness is of value in every way, as it holds promise for the present life and also for the life to come. The saying is sure and worthy of full acceptance. . . . Command and teach these things. Let no one despise your youth, but set the believers an example in speech and conduct, in love, in faith, in purity. (1 Tim. 4:7-12)

The youthful pursuit of the faith today is nothing new or surprising. What is different is our surprise that so many alternative proposals and options are available for the taking. The adult Christian community has forgotten that the early church thrived amidst a circus of cults in Greece and Rome and was to have staggering success, growth, and extension surrounded by a hostile and entrenched system. Acts 17:22 is one of the most vivid illustrations of that Christian/cultic encounter. And a large measure of the young church's success was its attractiveness and appeal to secular youth.

The Rediscovery of the Family

Is the American home and the traditional family terminal in this century? What about the epidemic proportions of divorce? Does the American public value the importance of the family, and is it even aware of the spiritual sources of strength that promote stability and vitality among its members?

The Role of Religion in the Home

In the past decade, articles, essays, and newspaper feature stories have argued that the traditional family structure in Western civilization is on the wane. Sociologists have been saying that the weakening of the family may be a sign that its values and heritage within American life will soon come to an end. Certainly more and more children are being raised in one-parent homes. Government statistics of late indicate that 50 percent of the youngsters born this year will probably grow up in a one-parent household.

In response to these developments, we sought to answer the questions which naturally form around such realities, e.g.: Do Americans still place a high premium on family life? And, do American parents need help in both spiritual and non-spiritual matters? Are parents actively seeking help in the raising of their children, or have they become satisfied in passing the burdens of childrearing to the schools and churches of this country?

Also, what is actually being pursued in the American home regarding religious activities and practices as taught and demonstrated by parents right now? What has been the impact of religion in the strengthening of family ties and aiding youngsters today to face the problems of the latter years of the twentieth century? To probe for the answers to these questions, the Gallup organization went to American parents themselves, recognizing that they would be the starting point for any legitimate discussion on these concerns.

It is apparent to most readers by now that countless families in the United States need help desperately, and the need for spiritual help is paramount. The majority of our reports indicate that many Americans belong to the "not quite Christian" category: They believe, but without strong convictions. They want the fruits or reward of faith, but seem to dodge the responsibilities and obligations. They say that they are Christian but often without a visible connection to a congregation or religious fellowship. The major challenge appears to be a task for the churches as well—how to guide men and women into becoming mature Christian personalities.

It is correct that many within our society have proposed that the facts of family life tell us that the traditional home is on the skids, that the increase in single homes, cohabitation, "team marriages," divorce, and single parents may be the clear signs that the American family is about to go under. Yet, two basic items keep surfacing in the most recent studies that have been compiled. First, the American people (including young adults) continue to be remarkably traditional in their value system, particularly regarding the importance of family ties; second, these same people are highly religious in their world-view.

The returns on the question of whether or not Americans are becoming disenchanted with family life are a bit surprising: the percentage of adults who say they are *satisfied* with their family life has *increased* over the last five years, with approximately three in four now expressing such satisfaction. In contradiction to the dire predictions by some sociologists that the breakdown of the nuclear family is at hand, responses to poll questions indicate that the majority of American women see marriage, home, and family as the ideal life-style for them. Three women in four in the United States say that marriage and children are among the important elements that would create the ideal life for them now and in the future. Of those women who would opt for marriage and children, 44 percent state flatly that they would prefer not to have a job outside the home while 32 percent would include a full-time, outside job as the ideal blueprint for a future life-style.[1]

This most recent report indicates the stereotypical "career girl" life—the image of being single, free, and in pursuit of a full-time career—has little appeal for the American woman, at least as a permanent way of social existence. In our studies, only 9 percent say they would prefer this as their main option in life. (This is not to say this preference will not grow and enlarge, but present percentages remain low.)

One of the largest majorities recorded in the family discussion survey—91 percent of the American people—would welcome emphasis on traditional family ties in the years ahead. This group included an overwhelming number of the young adults surveyed, and young people did not take a casual view of divorce, either. From every indication we have seen, the American public is voting in favor of the classic, traditional family—in their future hopes and dreams as well as in their near past history. The vast majority of North Americans see the family as the cornerstone of society and the best hope for a positive future. C. S. Lewis caught this mood in another time when he wrote:

> The home must be the foundation of our national life. It is there, all said and done, that character is formed. It is there that we appear as we really are. It is there we can

---

[1]"Religion in the Home: Education, Inspiration and Formation." An Address by George Gallup, Jr., given to the National Seminar of the Christian Life Commission of the Southern Baptist Convention, Orlando, Fl., March 26-28, 1979.

fling aside the wary disguises of the outer world and be ourselves. It is there that we retreat from the noise and stress and temptation and dissipation of daily life to seek the sources of fresh strength and renewed purity.

While the American man or woman gives the family an overwhelming vote of confidence and individual affirmation, there can be no denying the fact that the family is seriously threatened by dangerous forces at every side. In *Christianity Today,* Virginia Stern Owens has written, "It seems we know how to do almost everything else in this country except how to make lasting marriages and raise children." Census data and survey data would reinforce her concern. The divorce rate has doubled in the last ten years. Two in five children born in this decade will live in a single-parent home.

Another revealing response relating to the home (as developed by the Gallup-Kettering studies): each year in the last decade, discipline has been cited by parents in this country as the top problem facing the schools in their communities. Hundreds of teachers are physically attacked each month by their students. Thousands of school children are also physically abused. A recent Gallup Youth Survey indicated that as many as one teenager in five is fearful of bodily injury during school hours.

The serious problem of alcohol and drug abuse is cited by most parents as being the major difficulty currently being faced by youth in their communities. In fact, teenagers, themselves, name alcohol and drug abuse among the top problems facing their generation.

While we may be alarmed at the prevalence of alcohol and drug abuse among children and teenagers, we should not be so surprised because we learn from our surveys that four in ten parents who themselves drink have set no rules or guidelines for drinking among their offspring.

In addition, the teenage population of America appears to be in a quandary regarding sex. One result of this is that the United States is now dealing with an epidemic of teenage pregnancies. The information available points to a whole new set of attitudes toward sex developing among the majority of teenagers. These changing attitudes could have a deleterious effect on family life in the immediate future.

Some explain the problems of teenagers by proposing that young people are victims of national crosscurrents, particularly the weakening of family life through poor household communications, the mobility in our society which brings sudden geographic change, the influence of television, and the fact that grandparents no longer live in the same households with their children and grandchildren. The last item represents an unfortunate trend, for most readers are aware of the remarkable affinity between young and old. As Arnold Toynbee once said, "Grandparents and grandchildren are allies against a common enemy."

It is true that one of the key reasons for the threatened dissolution of the family unit is that while rearing children may be the most vital role a person can exercise in life, preparation for this task is greatly lacking. Adults plunge into marriage and raise children without the advance knowledge required to do a satisfying job. The learning is basically by trial and error.

The general decline in the quality of family life is signalled by a loss of values, aimless wandering in the world of secular pursuits, and an almost professional consumerism. Spiritual values were long ago eroded, and John Catoir concluded in the *Catholic Digest* that "for too many people, their own satisfaction is of supreme importance to them. God is not in the place of highest honor. This kind of individualistic thinking will usually subvert a relationship."

It is not surprising that many of the problems confronting families today could be traced in some measure to the decline in the proportion of Americans who say that religion is "very important" in their lives—from 75 percent in 1952, to 70 percent in 1965, and then another drop to 53 percent as of this writing. These downtrends parallel the proportion of Americans who say they received religious training in their youth—94 percent in 1952, 91 percent in 1965, and 83 percent in 1979.

The decline in religious training is of course related to the breakdown of religious communication within the family unit. When the long-term family survey was designed, we observed three interrelated elements in the religious upbringing of children, which we chose to call *religious education, inspiration,* and *formation.* It is our contention that none of these elements can be neglected or ignored if mature Christians are to develop in this generation.

Religious education is the basis for faith. Earlier surveys have provided the evidence that many parents as well as their children are spiritual illiterates. Many professed Christians can articulate in only the most clumsy fashion the significance of the resurrection of Jesus Christ for the world. While most have Bibles in their home, many have been unable to channel the teaching of Scripture into their lives. Many are unable to even name the four Gospels of Matthew, Mark, Luke, and John.

Religious inspiration is seen as a vital link to education. It has been well said that "religion is better caught than taught." We know that it is not enough to tell a child that she or he must go to church when the parent is unwilling to do the same. It seems appropriate that the focus on the family's religious life should deal with *shared* religious activities as well as the teaching of faith in the home.

Religious formation is regarded as a primary element in the religious training of children and youth. Christianity is a growth process. One monastery that flourished in the Middle Ages was known for a phrase with which the community began each day. Their phrase was, "Let us begin again to be Christians." It may be that in our own time too much emphasis has been placed on the "day that I found Christ" rather than the "day after." Christian conversion is the beginning but hardly the conclusion for those serious about becoming full and complete in the Lord.

Experts in the field of religious development contend that the growth process in the life of the spirit should not and cannot be forced. In *Your Growing Child and Religion,* R. S. Lee states:

Religious ideas can be taught but the truth of religion can only be discovered; and it is far more important to foster the spirit of discovery—which is the response to the challenge to adventure—than to persuade adolescents to accept without question what their teachers tell them.

We should in many cases go so far as to encourage an active distrust, at least a questioning, of the accepted religious beliefs. Only so will these become strong enough, and enough part of the person, to be able to stand the tests to which they will be subjected by everyday life in the world; and only so will they become a taking-off point for further progress into the realm of the spirit.

Barbara Morgan, member of the Word of God, a Christian community in Ann Arbor, Michigan, writes:

Because a child's spiritual life is wide-open, there's no limit to what God can do in his relationship with him. A child approaches God quite freely and naturally, without fears and doubts, and without the burden of a lifetime of sin. We should resist the temptation to measure our child against other Christian children or to mold our child into our image of a young Christian. God's relationship with each child is unique.

We should keep uppermost in our minds the fact that God is the potter and we are the hands. We don't know what the pot is going to look like, we simply have to respond to the potter. If we allow the Lord to establish his plan for our children, he will be able to shape each child into a masterpiece far more beautiful and enduring than any we could design.

One survey we conducted was designed to focus on these three elements in religious training and to shed light on the following questions:

1. *How important is the home in the religious training of children?* Does the continuing outcry over the removal of prayers from public schools indicate that parents think schools should play a greater role? Or do parents feel that Sunday school teachers should be chiefly responsible for the religious training of youth?

These are important questions, for if America's parents are not in agreement that the home is most important in the religious training of youth, a whole new set of approaches will be required. The current survey, however, indicates that 75 percent of parents say the home is the *most* important, 16 percent name the church, and 3 percent say the school. The prevailing opinion among all groups and faiths and in all regions of the country is that the home is the key factor in the religious and spiritual development of children.

2. *What* is *actually going on in the homes of Americans in terms of religious practices and activities—most importantly* shared *practices and activities?*

One cannot exaggerate the importance of *shared* experiences, of a child's having the undivided attention of a parent. Columnist William Shannon writes, "A young child needs a one-to-one emotional relationship with a loving adult if the child is to grow into a stable self-confident person."

In our survey, parents of children under 18 years old who live in the same household were asked whether or not they had done the following, in the previous seven days, with their children: said grace at meals, attended church services, attended other church-related activities, read the Bible together, talked about God and religion with their children, watched or listened to religious programs on TV or radio with their children. Here are the findings:

—42 percent of parents said grace before meals with their children

—38 percent attended church services with their children

—28 percent attended church-related activities with their children

—17 percent of parents read the Bible together with their children

—44 percent of parents talked about God and religion with their children

—31 percent of parents prayed or meditated with their offspring

—23 percent watched or listened to religious programs on TV or radio.

3. *What is the impact of religion on the home?* Is it strengthening family relationships? Is it helping children deal with the problems in their lives?

Looking at trends in America today—the divorce rate, the epidemic of alcohol abuse, the rise in unwanted pregnancies, and vandalism in the schools—one is tempted to answer, "very little." But the survey findings do give us at least some cause for encouragement:

—45 percent of parents say religion in their home has strengthened family relationships "a great deal"

—32 percent of parents say religion has helped their

children "a great deal" in dealing with the
problems in their lives
—Fewer than 10 percent say religion has *not* helped the
family situation at all.

Here is at least some testimony to the success of
churches' efforts to bring religion into the home and to
provide spiritual help for families. There is still further
survey evidence that religion does, indeed, make a
difference. Persons who fit the category of "very
religious"—making allowance for educational level
and other factors—tend to be happier, more goal-
oriented, and have a higher level of achievement.

Current survey findings, while encouraging in one
respect, can nevertheless be looked at in a different light:
—55 percent of parents say religion in the home has
strengthened family relations only "somewhat,"
"hardly at all," or "not at all," while 68 percent
of all parents say religion has helped their
children deal with their problems only "somewhat," "hardly at all," or "not at all."

In broad outline, then, these findings indicate the
tremendous challenge facing the clergy and other
religious leaders in this country. Looking to the future,
however, we can gain encouragement from survey
findings which show that homes where religion plays a
central role today are producing persons whose future
homes in turn will in all likelihood be religiously
oriented.

Examining, for example, the religious practices
and attitudes of parents surveyed who said that
religion was "very important" in their homes when
they were growing up, we see that their current level

of shared religious activities is very high. For instance, seven in ten parents in this group say they have read the Bible with their children at least once in the seven-day period tested. Sixty-three percent of parents whose upbringing was "very religious" say religion has greatly strengthened family relationships, while 62 percent of this group feel that religion is helping their children a "great deal" in regard to promoting spiritual growth.

New and creative efforts to "help families" are urgently needed, because the 1980s could well be a decade of severe dislocations in society unless we are able to deal with certain basic problems: unemployment among youth, which breeds crime and lawlessness; alcohol and drug abuse; voter apathy; and a lack of deep religious commitment.

What may be required is a new "team effort" between parents and clergy to deepen spiritual values in the home. Certain problems such as alcohol abuse call for immediate attention. The nation's churches, which have contact on a regular basis with half of the U.S. population, have a unique opportunity to help with the problem of alcohol abuse, particularly in the area of prevention.

Such a "team effort" between parents and teachers is now occurring and could be considered to be one of the most important developments in education in recent years. For years, parents have generally been content to dump all the problems of childrearing at the door of the school. Now, shocked by certain trends in society and in schools, parents are ready and eager to work closely with teachers. Many say that they would like to come to the schools to discuss with teachers problems related to discipline, drug and alcohol use, as well as educational problems.

What sort of joint efforts between parents and *clergy* could be developed out of the nation's churches? Here are some suggestions:

1. Programs could be developed to teach parents how to provide moral and religious training for their children. (The "case history" approach should be considered since a vicarious experience is as close as we can come to actual experience which is the real teacher.)

2. Perhaps more programs could be developed that bring parents and children together. The Church of Jesus Christ of Latter-day Saints has been remarkably successful with their Monday-night program. Here parents and children put everything else aside and worship in the context of programs that have been carefully tested. In a recent study on the American weekend, we audited the religious activities that people participate in on Sunday. The study confirms the fact that the Sabbath has lost much of its earlier meaning—people are spending their time shopping, watching pro football on TV, taking Sunday drives, but very little prayer (other than at church), very little Bible reading, very little meditation or prayerful reflection takes place.

    Perhaps Sunday might be given a new family significance in the Christian community as a whole just as Monday night is special for members of The Church of Jesus Christ of Latter-day Saints.

3. There is great room for the creation of television programs with powerful moral themes (without

being moralistic). We find in surveys that a remarkable number of Americans of all faiths, particularly younger Americans, are more profoundly moved by plays with a religious theme—television shows and movies, such as "Jesus of Nazareth"—than by the Bible stories they have heard or the sermons to which they have listened. The churches of America clearly have not taken full advantage of radio, television, movies, and theater in trying to enrich the spiritual life of Americans.

4. Another activity that currently has great appeal with American teenagers of both sexes is the religious retreat. In Poland it is popular to attend an "oasis." Nearly half of all American boys and girls express an interest in going on retreats. What better way to nourish the spiritual life of Americans and to tighten family bonds than for parents and children to go on retreats together?

Team efforts between parents and clergy will increase communications within the Christian family, for the secret of strong family ties rests in good communication, rooted in love and Christ.

A recent publication of Christophers Society notes:

Person-to-person family communication, verbal and nonverbal, means an exchange at all levels. It reinforces in each family member the message each needs in order to grow as an individual within the family. At the deepest level, that message is: "You are lovable and I love you. I need you. I need to be loved."

Good News for Catholics Is Good News for All Christians

The conflict/crisis mood which jarred the Roman Catholics a decade ago has yielded to a new flowering of the faith and a new confidence about being a Catholic Christian in America. Controversial issues such as divorce, abortion, and ordination of women remain. Yet trends seem to signal a golden era of growth and power ahead.

Among the most dramatic changes taking place in religion in America are those relating to the Catholic church. For the last decade the very opposite would seem to have been true as an almost endless litany of controversy, disruption, and apparent disintegration showered the landscape. The news ten years ago was bad, worse, and then catastrophic: priests were leaving the religious life faster than they could be counted;

57

seminary enrollment fell off the charts; congregational membership was in a permanent swoon; parochial schools were closing and selling at fifty cents on the dollar. And within the debates over dogma, doctrine, and discipline there was nothing but continual stress and unrelenting gloom. Much of the general uproar would eventually center on the acceptance or rejection of the pope as the church's absolute leader and a vigorous dialogue regarding the efficacy of the church's sexual ethic.

Today these questions have not vanished nor are they forever solved for the men and women—some 48 million—who comprise the Roman Catholic Church in North America. But a vital new spirit is flowing through the Catholic community. The conflict/crisis mood of a decade ago has yielded to a new flowering of the faith and a new confidence about being a Catholic in America. How has this come about, and is it likely to *continue?*

The first thing to note is that the Catholic population now is growing significantly in America. Ten years ago Catholics (18 and older) made up 25 percent of the national census; today they are at 28 percent and climbing. Among the many factors that contribute to this phenomenon is the relatively high birth rate and marked influx of Hispanics. Cubans, Puerto Ricans, and Mexican and Spanish Americans now comprise nearly 12 million people in America and are easily the largest minority within the Catholic church.

The proportion of young adult Catholics, those from

18–29 years old, is higher than parallel groups within Protestantism. Within this age group there has been a new surge in educational and income achievements as seen in a stronger representation of Catholics in business, government, and the professions. Mention of the leadership of the Catholic community in American political life leads many to think fondly of John F. Kennedy, the first Roman Catholic to gain the White House. Yet the major advances for Catholics holding political office have followed the Kennedy years in Washington. In 1967 there were thirteen Roman Catholics in the Senate, and the same number in 1977. But the number in the House for the same period jumped from 22 to 27. Among governors, the change has been most apparent—from 18 to 30.

Church attendance may be seen as a key barometer to the vitality of any religious group. We know that in the late 60s, following the reforms of Vatican II, attendance at Mass plunged, not to steady itself until the mid-70s. Now an upturn is seen in attendance, especially among the nation's youngest Catholic adults—18–29, a jump of 10 percent in two years! These gains are recorded during a time when the Catholic population, young and middle-aged alike, has grown increasingly liberal in mind and generous in spirit, especially in its attitudes toward key issues facing the church. This is, again, not just a weather aberration but rather a climate change, affecting not just the next county but an entire continent. Perhaps the comment of *US News and World Report* lends some light on the adjustment being made.

No longer do dissenting Catholics feel compelled to drop or join another faith. Instead, most are staying in the Church to thrash out with the hierarchy such painful issues as birth control, divorce, and new modes of worship.

And the feeling of working things out, being at home in America, and enjoying the fruits of ecumenism have all contributed to a new sense of well-being. In 1975 when Catholics were asked on a national survey to rate their own faith and how they felt about it, 62 percent said they felt "highly favorable." Just two years later, the same question to the same constituency brought out 69 percent declaring a highly favorable rating. With the amazing verve and global impact of John Paul II, the charts must be climbing higher again. To be young and Catholic in America is to feel good about oneself and the future.

There Are Problems

In the latest surveys of the most important problems facing Catholic families, the *economic* question was cited by one-third of the persons interviewed as being the *most* important. Money, finances, unemployment, cost of living, inflation, taxes—we all know the list—are bearing down hard on the religious community with older people assigning the greatest importance to these vexing problems. When people discuss other priority problems facing the family from the Catholic perspective, health, children's education, harmony in the home, are most frequently mentioned.

Yet there are people who seem to have found the proper balance between anxiety and euphoria, income and expenses, worry and confidence—some 30 percent said they had "No Problems"—at least not worth mentioning out loud.

When asked to separate the concerns facing Catholic families and the problems facing the institutional church, Catholic church members came right back to the topics and trauma of the early 60s—how to retain membership and grow; the abortion issue; too many changes, too fast; the church's stand on birth control; division in the church; decline in the number of priests and nuns; the church's stand on divorce. As we have noted, the primary issue of membership is directly related to many of the reforms initiated by Vatican II. When the old standbys of fish on Friday, Mass in Latin, saying the Rosary, predominance of parochial education, were sharply changed or changed altogether, many conservatives could not abide the new vision of church life. On the other hand, the Vatican's unwavering stance concerning sexual ethics and its opposition to birth control, abortion, and the re-marriage of divorced Catholics in the church seemed massively unyielding; liberals were under pressure to leave, and they slammed the door on the way out.

Many Catholics are remaining loyal to the church while they hammer out the answers to the questions of sexual ethics. Some 73 percent believe that lay people should be allowed to practice birth control by artificial means. Not a majority, but a large minority, 44 percent, argue that the Catholic church should relax its standards that forbid all abortions under any circumstances. Should divorced Catholics be permitted to remarry in the mother church? Yes, say 69 percent of the Roman Catholics in America. The people themselves are marking out the changes to come. Yet alterations of historic faith and practice are not as simple as taking a poll on the front steps of a suburban home. And while broad interpretations and practices and liberal reforms are supported by large numbers, there is a nostalgic look at the old Latin Mass. At least 64 percent within the Catholic communion of North America feel that it should still be permitted.

Signs of Ecumenism

One of the most powerful trends coursing through the Catholic church today is ecumenicity. The proposals of Pope John XXIII and the formation of Vatican II are having a healthy effect all over the world, and the influence is welcome in the Western hemisphere. When asked if the Catholic church should become *more* ecumenical, 84 percent of Catholics responded in the affirmative. When asked how they felt about Protestants in general, 87 percent expressed favorable sentiments toward their "separated brethren." The Protestant answer to the same question about Catholics was more restrained; some 73 percent said they held the Catholic church in favorable regard. Southern Protestants were the least enthusiastic in this poll.

Ecumenical models of cooperation and conversation continue to flourish, such as the dialogues between

Lutherans and Roman Catholics, Episcopalians and Roman Catholics, and Presbyterians and Roman Catholics. An interesting development from these conversations has been the joining of individual parishes through covenants, which The Reverend Thadeus Horgan, S.A., co-director of the Graymoor Ecumenical Institute and associate editor of *Ecumenical Trends,* describes as "an agreement between two or more local parishes or congregations coming from different traditions who pledge one another some degree of cooperation, support, and understanding."[1] Some of the practical advantages of these inter-parish partnerships are evident when congregations link to sponsor senior citizen clubs, day-care centers, or hospital and nursing home visitation. The third activity, understanding, implies perception and appreciation of each other's historic roots and present operative traditions. Debating, polemics, or convert-making are considered the opposite of the goal of understanding embodied in the inter-parish covenant.

The impulse and desire for Christian fellowship is being extended beyond the casual, infrequent events of inter-church cooperation and goodwill to very specific, observable happenings, such as the Ogden Covenant formed by St. Joseph's Roman Catholic Parish and the Good Shepherd Episcopal parish in Ogden, Utah. Established in 1977, the covenant is both idealistic and practical as two separated Christian communions explore a positive response to Jesus' prayer and invitation that "they all be one" (John 17:21).

---

[1] 8 (March 1979), 33.

The Ogden Covenant

In the Name of the Father, The Son, And the Holy Spirit. Amen.

Whereas, it is the Will of our Lord Jesus Christ "that they all may be one;" and

Whereas, the highest leadership of the Roman Catholic and Anglican Churches have expressed a desire for reunion of these Christian and Sister Churches; and

Whereas, the theologians of these Churches are meeting to solve the theological problems involved in reunion; and

Whereas, the Bishop of the Roman Catholic Diocese of Salt Lake City and the Bishop of the Episcopal Diocese of Utah have expressed approval of ecumenical dialogue; and

Whereas, the peoples of Saint Joseph's Church and the Church of the Good Shepherd, both in the City of Ogden, and the State of Utah, are conscious of the Will of Jesus Christ and the desire of their respective Churches for reunion;

Now,

Therefore we solemnly and reverently enter into this covenant for a period of two years and hereby pledge:

1. To pray for one another—including in our liturgies a petition for the reunion of these Churches as well as praying for each other here in Ogden.

2. To invite, from time to time, representatives from the parishes to attend the worship of the other, in hope of eventual sacramental unity.
3. To continue seasonal occasions of joint worship and dialogue.
4. To share as far as is feasible our facilities and programs.
5. To sponsor jointly an action project to benefit the Community of Ogden.
6. To work together for social justice and the Common Good.
7. To sponsor jointly cultural and social events when appropriate and possible.

We dedicate ourselves to these objectives and ask the blessing of Almighty God on this Covenant that we may be faithful to the agreement to His Honor and Glory.

The artistry of change is one area that needs exhaustive study within the Catholic community, for creative reform which leads millions of people from the convulsions of the sixties to the consolidations of the eighties is an art form, indeed. Looking at the wreckage of the Roman Church in America at the early point of 1972, sociologists William McCready and Andrew Greeley wondered if the Catholic church could have a viable future at all. Writing in the journal, *America,* in 1972, McCready and Greeley stated that "there is evidence of the coming apart of the traditional, tightly bound organization of the

Church . . . the loyalty is gone, the creativity is gone, and the meaning system is gone or, at least, going."[2]

There is no question that the appearance of Pope John XXIII in 1962 was one of the turning points not only for Catholics but also for the global Christian community. Pope John was elected by a slight majority. His advanced age prompted his designation as a "caretaker Pope" until the College of Cardinals could agree on a long-range policy and be led by a personality who met the needs of a broader constituency. Meanwhile, Pope John began acting in his own style—turning the papacy into a pastoral office, mixing with the classes and masses, and showing up in prisons and hospitals. He was known to have a motor scooter and a propensity for opening windows and airing out buildings. He did all of this and more. He had a vision of a great ecumenical council, gathering not only the princes of the church for new thought, visions, and surprises, but inviting the Protestants to send observers, to encourage the Catholic community to be in fellowship with all brethren, separated though they might now be. But more, he loved all humankind as Christ's vicar; he felt himself to be their humble servant and extended the graciousness and love of his faith to "all people of goodwill." Pope John XXIII shook a branch of Christendom and the whole world felt pleasant vibrations. The artistry of change was not a theory, not some quiet committee report, but the moving of God's Spirit through a man and church which were ready.

---

[2]"The End of American Catholicism," 127 (October 28, 1972), 337-8.

When the active but separated progressive groups within Catholicism saw this powerful laser light being transmitted from Rome, they knew that the hour had come for massive, meaningful change. The rigid hierarchical structure began to yield in a variety of ways—out-moded rituals and attire were the first to undergo change. Nuns began to dress in contemporary clothing, masses were heard in English, and the laity was heard on Sundays as well as Holy Days. A great springtime entered the church, and though the first fresh currents created dangerous turbulence, the results would be cleansing and exhilarating.

Protestants were deeply affected by a new vision of Rome. All the old quarrels, prejudices, and favorite Catholic put-downs had to be reviewed. Catholics and Protestants were now free to love each other and rediscover their great bonds of commonality while permitting themselves the luxury of debate and disagreements without rock-throwing or name-calling. The reaching out to one another as Christians has generated many important events, conversations, and inquiries. Eighty-four percent of the Catholics surveyed said they wanted more ecumenical overtures on the part of their church. They expressed a need for more information on other faiths, as well as various Protestant denominations, and many wished to have the basis of their common agreement with other Christians spelled out so that the feasibility of prayer groups and Bible study together could be examined.

The harvest from the ecumenical vineyard is being gathered by both Catholics and Protestants. To the Protestant church it brings enrichment of liturgy—a new emphasis on the Lord's Supper, the prayers and responses of the people, and more familiarity with vestments and banners heralding the different periods of the liturgical year. For Catholics, it has brought a return to the Bible as central in study, personal devotions and liturgy, a revival in the role of preaching in the life of the church, and a surge in music, choirs, and congregational singing.

When *U.S. Catholic* took a national survey of some 18,000 Catholic parishes, some unique features about present-day practices emerged that seem to come straight out of the nearest Methodist, Lutheran, or Baptist programs. Catholics had regular prayer groups, reported 45 percent of those polled. A large 61 percent said they had Bible study on a regular basis. Women were being asked to be lectors in Mass in 86 percent of the churches while 47 percent said that women members were distributing communion elements in the parish.

Music in the Catholic church is on the rise. Seventy-four percent of the parishes report that a choir is regularly used; 58 percent have a guitar or folk choir participating in the Mass and worship services. This may account for the young adult and youth participation which is growing and being heard in the parish precincts. But the kind of music and the type of hymns presently in vogue are driving some church people speechless or songless. Writes John Mahoney,

> Many Catholics and ex-Catholics seem to think that the congregational singing of painfully bad hymns is an integral part of the new liturgy. The wet blanket of bad

hymns thrown over the congregation is what the faithful have encountered since the old mass became the New Mass. How could they know that this was not the way it was meant to be? . . . The hymns are terrible! The melodies are dreary and uninspired. The key they are played in causes strain and ache in the vocal chords. . . . Most people around me do not sing or at most mumble the hymn inaudibly. . . . I sometimes wonder if disgust with contemporary church singing is not one factor turning people away from attendance at Mass.[3]

Preaching is gaining a more significant role in the Catholic church, but problems are not absent in this area either. Catholic writer James Breig has said that too many sermons in his denomination are known as bulldozers—bull from the pulpit and dozers from the people! He interviewed five leading preachers within the Catholic communion for *U.S. Catholic* to hear their suggestions for better preaching of the Word.[4] All agreed that "the essential ingredient of a good sermon is the person delivering it. Without a committed, involved, prepared, Gospel-oriented priest, a homily is doomed."

Father William Toohey, C.S.C., director of the Campus Ministry at Notre Dame University, proposed that

preaching today will be successful when it imitates the style Jesus himself found successful. Jesus took

---

[3]"Sour Notes About Parish Music," *U.S. Catholic* (April 1978), 41.

[4]Father Henry Fehren, "Let's Clap for Good Sermons" (April 1978), 14-18.

something very graphic, very familiar to his people—a mustard seed—and used it to connect with something unseen. . . . We have to do the very same thing today, using the experience of our people. The preacher has to ask himself: What movies are people seeing? What T.V. are they watching? What are they talking about?

Father Henry Fehren, noted Catholic author and journalist, says that it is up to the priest

to know Scripture and theology and to present Christ to the people. Sermons should be getting better these days, for there are many institutes and workshops to help clergy up-date their understanding of Scripture and there are many homiletical services from which to draw ideas.

When *U.S. Catholic* asked their readers to suggest ideas to improve preaching in the churches, a rich and surprising group of answers were approved:

1. Sixty-nine percent said that good sermons should be applauded.
2. Lay people should be allowed to preach, so said a majority of replies.
3. Churches should have the nerve to publish a schedule of who preaches at which Mass so that parishioners could follow their favorites.
4. A majority of 62 percent believe that there should be sermons about money, but the bulk of those replying feel that annually is often enough!
5. While 63 percent say that they are frequently or always satisfied with the Sunday sermon they hear, 83 percent do not want it to stretch beyond twenty minutes.

   6. Most daring of all, 73 percent of the parishioners
       would like to have a pew card on which they could
       comment on individual sermons.

Lay participation is another area of change in the
Catholic church today. Lay readers and lay preachers
will become more active, not less, in Roman circles.
There is not only the interest but the need to have laity
in key parish positions—paid or volunteer. Many
priests today find themselves to be the sole professional
in a parish of 1,500 or 2,000 households. Only as the
laity begin to fulfill leadership/ministerial roles can the
church look again to expansive outreach in the name of
Christ.

Vatican II, again, is the source of inspiration and
direction in these matters, making it imperative to
involve the laity in the central acts of the church, even
to the possibility of ordaining women and married
people. In the article on the laity from the Vatican II
Constitution of the Church, the new role model is
described:

> The laity are by reasons of the knowledge, competence,
> or outstanding ability they may enjoy, permitted, and
> sometimes even obliged to express their opinions on
> those things that concern the good of the church. Let it
> always be done in truth, in courage, and in prudence.

In the act of encouraging and supporting the advance of
the laity this same document proclaims,

> A great many good things are to be hoped for from this
> familiar dialogue between the laity and their pastors. In

the laity a strengthened sense of personal responsibility, a renewed enthusiasm, a more ready application of their talents to the projects of their pastors. The latter, on the other hand, aided by the experience of the laity, can more clearly and more aptly come to decisions regarding both spiritual and temporal matters. In this way the whole church, strengthened by each one of its members, may more effectively fulfill its mission for the life of the world.

In addition to the healthy exchange between Catholics and Protestants in the arena of church life, the recognition of common values and concerns, shared ethical teachings, and programs of social and political advocacy provide opportunity for united ministries.

For example, the most recent Gallup surveys indicate that few problems are of greater concern to both Protestant and Catholic parents than the widespread use and abuse of drugs, alcohol, and tobacco among teenagers. Here is an area in which religious bodies can work together to provide guidance for youth.

The involvement of minorities in the church is another realm of shared concern for Catholics and Protestants. Gallup studies reveal that the Catholic church has the highest acceptance and encouragement of blacks in their worship services. Sixty percent of Catholic congregations studied are integrated. Current statistics for Protestants show a lower percentage of integrated churches; only 40 percent of Protestant churches nationally have integrated Sunday worship.

Presbyterians have the highest percentage of integrated worship services among Protestants—51 percent. The Episcopal Church is on the lower end of the scale with integration at 34 percent, but it is highest in seeking to welcome more blacks to services with 70 percent responding positively to that question. These statistics suggest that there will be continued success in Presbyterian-Roman Catholic and Episcopal-Catholic dialogue.

Other joint efforts might center on mutual hunger programs, shared Bible study activities, community outreach to prisons and state hospitals, and task forces to deal with the problem of violence on television.

Currently the greatest conflict in Protestant-Catholic dialogue revolves around the issues of abortion, artificial birth control, homosexuality, and divorce. A helpful paper dealing with these potential conflicts for the followers of Christ came out of a Roman Catholic, Reformed, and Presbyterian consultation meeting in Richmond, Virginia, in 1971. In considering a joint statement on ministry within the church, the participants noted that one object of ministry "is to help each Christian do the truth in love." Reviewing the work on the consultation, church historian Dr. J. A. Ross MacKenzie felt this statement to be incisive:

> None of our churches considers the way one lives as a matter of indifference for the Christian faith. At the same time, within every church there exist wide differences regarding moral standards for judging what is right and wrong, what is just and unjust, what is charity of Christ and what is opposed to it.

Dr. MacKenzie suggests that resolution of conflict for Christians seeking to reconcile their sharp differences over ethical practices can be found when two questions are answered. The first question that all parties should ask is—What has been the traditional or customary moral reflection and action? In other words, from what sources and reservoirs have Christians drawn when developing and shaping new moral perspectives?

In his own reply to the first question, Dr. MacKenzie quotes from the work of Scottish New Testament scholar Robin Barbour, who once classified the sources of ethical guidance which directed the stance of the early Christian church in the first century:

1. The ethical framework of the Hebrew society as understood in the Torah and seen in the teachings of Christ;
2. The moral teaching of the secular world with particular awareness of the Greek philosophers;
3. The words, deeds, and example set by Jesus himself as translated throughout his life and ministry—a ministry of such strength and love that it informs and transforms everything.

The second question quickly arrives: "Are these elements still adequate for helping Christians to do the truth?" asks Ross MacKenzie. Our perplexity and confusion grows because we are living in a new hour and covering a new ethical landscape devoid of signs, directions, and sure-footed guides. MacKenzie notes that the implication of arms trade, SALT agreements, international boycotts, currency upheavals, discoveries in genetics and biology help to increase the confusion and bewilderment of Christian ethical absolutes.

But this may be a source of good news for Christians and a new bonding of Protestants, Catholics, and Orthodox to each other as they address the topics that at first confound. "The very turmoil," says MacKenzie,

> may actually, in the end, aid in producing a larger sense of unity in Christ. This very weakness in being able to address a clear word to the moral questions of the late-twentieth century may ultimately draw the churches closer together and move them to identify, although tentatively and with caution, what it means for the Christian to do the truth in love.[5]

One of the continuing requests that Roman Catholics make of their leaders is a way of becoming more familiar and knowledgeable about the brother and sister churches within Christendom. Aside from the expected short summaries that reference books provide and the abbreviated paragraphs that comparative religion handbooks offer on the topic, there is not an overwhelming body of current material. Knowing this, Catholics and their friends may wish to ponder the steady flow of documents that are produced by the consultations between the Roman Catholic Church and dozens of other denominations and branches of Christianity. (These consultations are not exclusively Christian—there are Jewish and Moslem dialogues in

---

[5]*Ecumenical Trends* (March 1979), published by Graymoor Ecumenical Institute, Garrison, N.Y. 10524.

progress—revealing the depth and staying power of the ecumenical movement.) While some of these papers, speeches, and publications in scholarly journals appear ponderous and rather academic, they do reveal the current temperature of inter-faith conversations, and their deliberate style need not disguise the levels of agreement and the areas of unresolved conflict.

The Orthodox-Roman Catholic consultation in the United States is a strong illustration of the need for dialogue among Christians, particularly those with ancient separations and a history of what might best be described as a family theological quarrel. Both communions are represented by visionary and articulate spokesmen: the Roman Catholics by William Cardinal Baum, Archbishop of Washington, D.C.; and the Most Reverend Iakovos, Greek Orthodox Archbishop of North and South America and Archbishop of New York.

A document on the sanctity of marriage is the most recent one released by the consultation representing the two Christian bodies. It is pithy, theological, and filled with supportive arguments to reinforce the value of a Christian marriage. In part it says:

> At a time when the sacred character of married life is radically threatened by contrary lifestyles, we the members of the Orthodox-Roman Catholic Consultation feel called by the Lord to speak from the depth of our common faith and to affirm the profound meaning, the glory, and honor of married life in Christ.

The document goes on to state that for both Christian churches, marriage is a sacrament, and through the prayers and actions of our wedding rites we profess the presence of Christ in the Spirit and believe that it is the Lord who unites a man and woman in a life of mutual love. In this sacred union, husband and wife are called by Christ to not only live and work together, but also to share their Christian life so that each with the aid of the other may progress in the life of holiness and so achieve Christian perfection.

There is not a higher view of marriage available to humankind than the words just printed. They are powerful and compelling words; and to a society sick of casual alliances and plagued by insincere, childish unions built on pleasure and barely refined selfishness, they present a clear and shining alternative for true and lasting marriages. The statement goes on to affirm that Christian marriages not only bring joy and love to the couple, but "by total sharing with each other, seek their own growth in holiness and that of their children and thus show forth the presence on earth of God's kingdom."

The two major Christian communions then deal with their different approaches to a Christian marriage's greatest threat: divorce. Their thoughts are brief and succinct: "Both the Orthodox and Roman Catholic churches affirm the permanent character of Christian marriage: 'What God has joined together, let no man put asunder' (Matthew 19:6)." However, the Orthodox Church, out of consideration of human realities, permits divorces, after the church exhausts all possible efforts to save the marriage, and tolerates remarriages in order to avoid further human tragedies. The Roman

Catholic Church recognizes the dissolution of sacramental non-consummated marriages either through
solemn religious profession or by papal dispensation.
To resolve the personal and pastoral issues of failed
marriages which have been consummated, an inquiry is
often undertaken to uncover whether there existed
some initial defect in the marriage covenant which
would render the marriage invalid.

The marriage statement of the two sister churches
concludes with the admission that their common faith
concerning the sanctity of marriage has not yet
resolved the pastoral problems of Orthodox-Catholic
wedding celebrations nor the issue of the religious
upbringing of children from such a union.

The secularist may be puzzled by all this, the inactive
member indifferent; but to the faithful of both
churches, these are real questions surfacing again and
again in a real world which God loves. What makes any
of this work is the confidence that both groups have in
the guidance of the Holy Spirit. And as Martin Luther
said, "The Holy Spirit is a happy Spirit."

The Unchurched Christian in America-Faith Without Fellowship

If anything, the unique study on which this chapter is based reveals that the unchurched are believers. They pray. They believe in Jesus Christ. They think seriously about life after death. They trust the resurrection story of Easter morning. They want their children to have religious instruction. In fact, with a few variations, the unchurched claim the same turf as the churched—except they are not attending, supporting, or belonging to a congregation of the visible church. One encouraging sign, though, is the fact that more than half express a positive feeling about the institutional religious community.

One of the most enterprising projects to date concerning the unchurched American was a poll and study sponsored by some thirty-one organizations and religious bodies. These findings, published in 1978, discovered that some 61 million American adults are not members of any church or religious institution. The churches involved wanted to consider their life-styles, beliefs, upbringing, training, and social/personal relations so they might respond more fully and openly to the needs of these people. The definition of an "unchurched" person in this study was an individual who is not a member of a church or synagogue or who has not attended a church or synagogue in the past six months. (Attendance at a funeral or wedding, or even participation at a special holiday, such as Yom Kippur, Christmas, or Easter did not qualify someone as being "churched.") Essentially the poll/study probed these questions:

- Who are the unchurched, and how do they differ from those who are churched?
- What factors lead to becoming unchurched?
- What can churches do to encourage the unchurched to become part of the community of active worshipers?

Early in the national study, it was absolutely clear that there were a number of deeply religious persons who were disaffiliated from the institutional church—some may have had health problems, others physical disabilities. (Robert Schuller has noted in his writings that many of his first drive-in church attenders were those who could not physically get in and out of a traditional church but could participate seated in their cars.)

The established statistics from this study are simple and clear: 41 percent of the adult population in North America are unchurched—61 million. These are people 18 and over. The churched group in the same age category is 59 percent or 89 million adults. (The U.S. Department of Labor's April, 1978, estimate of the total adult civilian non-institutionalized population is around 150,116,000.)

The kind of questions asked of both the churched and unchurched dealt with basic religious beliefs—the theological and philosophical factors in a person's life. It should be noted here that the survey results for Jews, Eastern Orthodox, and non-whites are not reported due to the relatively small sample base for each of these groups. Everyone was asked to identify his or her individual religious practices including prayer, Bible reading, church-going, and personal meditation.

The whole spectrum of values and goals in life, attitudes toward institutions in American life as well as the institutional church were probed and tallied. Travel, mobility, social status, activities on weekends and Sundays, plus the impact of radio and television are all part of this penetrating report. In the cliché of the hour, there is good news and bad news for everyone.

Attitudes and Values of the Churched and the Unchurched

A significant result of the survey information is the finding that there is nationwide acceptance of traditional values. While historians may tag the 1960s and the 1970s as the decades of revolt, protest, and disillusionment, the 1980s are already cited as a return to "normalcy." Both the churched and unchurched stated by large majorities that they would welcome "more emphasis on traditional family ties and more respect for authority." Both groups also were eager to see "more emphasis on working hard" (although a slightly higher proportion of the churched than the unchurched would do so). The return to traditional values for both groups is seen in the following breakdown:

- Nine in ten (89 percent) say they would welcome more respect and authority in the coming years.
- A similar proportion (91 percent) would welcome more emphasis on traditional family ties.
- Seven in ten (69 percent) say they would welcome more emphasis on working hard.
- Three out of every four (74 percent) would *not* like to see more acceptance of marijuana usage, and six in ten (62 percent) would be opposed to wider acceptance of sexual freedom.

In the search and return to historic values and traditions, there is some disagreement between the churched and unchurched in their attitudes and ethics. Of the twenty-two statements presented to both groups, the unchurched found this comment to be to their liking, or representative of their feelings: "The rules about morality preached in the churches and synagogues today are too restrictive." Generally, the unchurched are more likely to accept changes in personal ethics. For example, regarding extra-marital sex, the unchurched believe it is "always wrong" by 53 percent, while among the churched, the figure is 74 percent.

In their approach to daily life, 82 percent of the

churched in this survey say that they have clear-cut goals and a satisfying life purpose. Seventy percent of the unchurched could agree with this statement. The churched are more prone to say that "facing my daily tasks is a source of pleasure and satisfaction"; 87 percent of them concurred while 78 percent of the unchurched so stated.

This continent is filled with searchers and seekers of the true meaning of life. Many of them have pursued their identity and fulfillment in sports, recreation, entertainment, superficial sex, and shallow friend-ships. The hunger of the soul and the spiritual void enlarged by all these pursuits has created both a judgment and an opportunity for the churches, wherever they find themselves. Campus ministries, prison fellowships, hospital chaplaincies are swarming with seekers and searchers for religious depth and meaning. In response to a discussion about the role of the college chapel, a recent Princeton University graduate, Lyn Marie Albrecht, wrote:

The most serious lack in a religionless void is the inability to establish and nurture healthy human relationships. The fellowship inspired by social agree-ment in the deep and powerful levels of religious affiliation is necessary in an environment that thrives on competition and argumentation. (Anyone who has survived the combat and shelling of an Ivy education can feel the truth in that judgment. . . .) True intimacy and love at Princeton are much less highly valued than individual transcendence and psychological triumph. Standards of correct human relationships must be taught with the same emphasis as intellectual trivia. It is surprising how little insight into their own emotional and spiritual needs "brilliant" minds can have.[1]

The unchurched person and the unchurched family are caught in a permissive society that has no enforced standards regarding alcohol usage, sexual experimentation, and social responsibility. The true discipline for the mature individual is from within, and the unchurched person has discovered that the general tone of twentieth-century society is doing little to provide lasting ways of coping for the moral and spiritual person. A return to the church as a stable, enduring, and supportive society begins to look possible and hopeful to many of those polled. The response to the following question from the national survey seems pivotal. "Now think about your present attitude toward the church. Could there be a situation where you could see yourself becoming a fairly active member of a church or synagogue now?" (This was asked of those who were unchurched but had once been active in a religious affiliation.) Fifty-two percent gave an affirmative answer to this question, with only 13 percent saying "definitely not."

It is apparent in this study that churched and unchurched alike seek meaning in their lives and a clearer understanding of the values and traditions that bring sanity and stability to living. The church holds the promise of helping people to interpret life and to live better. There are stumbling blocks, however, for many

---

[1] "Letters to the Editor," *Princeton Alumni Weekly* (June 11, 1979), 8.

who desire this end. As we have seen, the unchurched often disagree wih the churched regarding social standards and find strict codes of conduct and dogmatic theology too restrictive. The churched, in turn, often regard the life-style of many of the unchurched as unacceptable for members of the religious community.

Attitudes Toward the Church

There is great hunger among the churched as well as the unchurched for a sharper focus on the primary questions of life. A large bloc of the unchurched seem to be saying that they would like to be part of a living fellowship that dealt directly and personally with the larger, more sensitive issues in our world. But 49 percent of the unchurched and 39 percent of the churched agreed with the statement that "Most churches and synagogues today are not effective in helping people find meaning in life." Closely related is the assessment of 56 percent of the unchurched that "most churches and synagogues today are too concerned with organizational as opposed to theological or spiritual issues." Church members agreed by 47 percent.

People have turned away from the church for a variety of personal reasons which are often variations on the theme of the church's distance from real life issues. In his book *Who Are the Unchurched?* J. Russell Hale quotes from several interviews with people who are disillusioned with the church. A former Methodist from Maine said:

I would say it was overexposure as a child. My parents were so involved. Their whole life was church activities. Just got so that every time my father turned around, he was back at church. I was pulled to church on a sled. There was a prayer meeting every Tuesday, WCTU on Wednesday, Ladies' Sewing Circle at the house. That was my whole life until my father died, that was all we knew.

It was just overexposure and developed in me this tremendous negative attitude—I got so I was bored to tears—so I just can't. I go occasionally, but I just hate it.[2]

A navy officer who served his country in Vietnam recalled his youth as a flower child and his feeling that his church life gave him no perspective on the problems he faced nor a world-view to deal with the war when it came.

I saw my buddies blown up by 12, 13, 14-year-old kids. I lost a little bit of my faith. Organized religion just didn't set well with me.

Now I see the Church as not much different from government—it's overpowering! Local people don't really have a voice in what happens to their money. They tend to perpetuate the system. . . . They just build buildings and take our money away from local needs. The cathedrals and the foreign missionaries are nice, but the Church has gotten to be a kind of power broker. That is not religion.

That is not what a church organization is for.[3]

---

[2](Glenmary Research Center, 1977), p. 55.
[3]*Ibid.*, p. 49.

An executive in southern California who had been long active in the national leadership of her denomination says:

> I think the churches have gotten like a lot of parts of society. They have to worry so much about paying the rent that they have forgotten the good news. They forget the evangelical message. They forget love. I find some of the clergy are very wonderful people, but a lot them have to seek out the almighty dollar so much . . . that they are robbing the people of the great heritage of the Church . . . the leaders are afraid of theology.[4]

Because they have been disappointed by the church or because they do not perceive a positive function for the church, many now argue for independence in determining their religious beliefs and practices. Eighty-six percent of the unchurched say they don't want beliefs dictated to them by the church. An artist in California interviewed by Hale comments:

> I believe that no religion or no person can tell me what my communication with God is. It is between God and me. . . . I don't care whether the Church accepts me or not. I accept myself, and I am higher than the Church. I am a child of God. . . . I'd like to be able to be a part of helping, understanding, giving my time to someone. If that is what my Church became, a part of me would be a part of that, because it is what God wants me to do. But,

---

[4]*Ibid.*, p. 46.

as long as it is going to be rules and punishment, "I'll slap your hand if you do this" or "You are out of the Church if you do that"—No, I'll never be a part of that.[5]

The reasons many people believe they have the Christian faith yet demonstrate no institutional fulfillment are to be found in the failure of the churches as well as among the unchurched themselves. The generally low level of spirituality, massive interest in busy work, buildings, and grounds, panting after necessary dollars, immunity to social distress, distance from so many of the alarms and anxieties of the poor and deprived, frequent frowning upon youth, are just some of the factors that have created a reaction against the established religious bodies in America. The reaction is seen in the response to this question from the poll: Do you think that a person can be a good Christian if he or she doesn't attend church? Eighty-eight percent of the unchurched gave a positive response to that inquiry, and 70 percent of the churched agreed that it was possible.

Another person interviewed by J. Russell Hale commented, "No, I don't think that membership means I'm a better Christian. I feel that we live perfectly good Christian lives as it is, and I think that we do good, and I don't think we have to be a member of the Church."[6]

---

[5] *Ibid.*, p. 47.
[6] *Ibid.*, p. 46.

Beliefs of the Unchurched
and the Churched

When we examine the beliefs of the churched and the unchurched concerning the major items of faith and personal theology, we are impressed with the *similarities* between these two groups. If you thought that a person who dropped out of congregational life and entered the ranks of the unchurched became a thoroughgoing secularist, without spiritual markings and bereft of religious persuasions, you would be informed by this study that no such condition exists! It is true that there are a host of pleasant pagans waving to you from across the street or ready to take their quiet Sunday drive to the shopping center across town. But they are in the distinct minority within the ranks and classification of the unchurched.

For, if anything, the unchurched are believers. They pray. They believe in Jesus Christ. They think about life after death. They trust the resurrection story of Easter morning. They want their children to receive religious instruction. In fact, with a few distinct variations, which are later on discussed, the unchurched claim the same turf as the churched—except they are *not* attending, supporting, or belonging to a congregation of the visible church.

Reviewing, studying, pondering this mass of material, one comes, at last, to this conclusion: The unchurched are overwhelmingly believers; and it is not loss of faith, in most cases, that has caused people to become unchurched. Dean Hoge, a sociologist of the Catholic University of America notes, "The proportion of Americans who are unchurched for philosophical reasons is not great. Other forces seem to be more determinative, such as interpersonal influences, community relationships, and lifestyles."[7]

Consider these statistics:

While nine in ten (89 percent) of the churched people believe that Jesus is God or the Son of God, no less than 64 percent of the unchurched believe the same truth.

While 93 percent of the churched affirm their faith in the resurrection of Jesus Christ, some 68 percent of these non-attenders, non-contributors, non-belongers, say they also believe in the resurrection of Christ.

While four out of five of the churched group say that they have made a personal commitment to Jesus Christ, no less than two out of five of the unchurched will make the same affirmation.

When we go next to the Bible and its authority in the lives of people, these statistics emerge: 46 percent of the churched people say that the Bible is the actual word of God, and "is to be taken literally, word for word." At least 27 percent of the unchurched would also agree with that orthodox statement. But look at this: Some 47 percent of the churched are more comfortable with this statement: "The Bible is the inspired word of God but not everything in it should be

---

[7]"The Unchurched American," study conducted for The Religious Coalition to Study Backgrounds, Values and Interests of Unchurched Americans, convened and coordinated by The National Council of Churches, U.S.A. by The Princeton Religion Research Center and The Gallup Organization, Inc., 1978, p. 10.

taken literally, word for word." Of the unchurched, 43 percent said this reflected their feelings about the Old and New Testaments. (Some 20 percent of the unchurched did state, however, that they thought the Bible to be simply "an ancient book of fables, legends, history, and moral preceptions recorded by men." Only 3 percent of the churched would feel comfortable with that view of Scripture.) Regarding religious instruction for their children, a surprising 75 percent of the unchurched state they would like to have a child of theirs receive such instruction—only 10 percent said no.

The whole realm of prayer, meditation, and communion with God, as reported in this finding, continues to enforce the fact that this is a very religious cosmos, that churched and unchurched turn to God frequently and expectantly and are alert to the value of religious experiences.

When discussing their personal prayer life, 98 percent of the churched group said that they prayed to God, while their distant spiritual cousins made a very strong 76 percent response: that they also prayed to God, and 45 percent of them allowed that they prayed once a day or more! These unchurched may be out of touch with institutions, religious communities, and congregational programs of worship, study, and fellowship; but they are not out of touch with their Creator. Both the churched (7 percent) and the unchurched (10 percent) indicated that they practiced specific techniques of meditation, e.g., as taught by T.M., Zen, or the Divine Light mission.

In this study the churched respondents said, by 43 percent, that they had a religious experience that was "a particularly powerful religious insight or awakening." The unchurched were much lower, with only 24 percent acknowledging such a moment. The process of revelation varied greatly: the churched persons who said yes went on to state that it was not a sudden but a gradual development—so said 64 percent. The unchurched who noted a religious awakening stated that it was sudden (some 56 percent in that reply), while 42 percent said it was gradual.

When using the popular term "born-again," the churched respondents were equally divided with 47 percent saying that they had had a "born-again experience that was an identifiable turning point" in their life. The others, 47 percent, said they had not had such an experience. Around 25 percent of the unchurched allowed that they had had a born-again experience; however, 67 percent responded negatively to this question.

We are impressed and somewhat surprised by the commonality of these two groups. Indeed, it must be something entirely different than the thelogical premises described which causes one group to be churched, active, supportive, and belonging and the other to be distant, removed, disconnected, inactive, and out of touch with a specific religious fellowship. Despite a mutuality of theological conviction and affirmation, the two groups diverge at the point of membership and attendance:

Are you, yourself, a member of a church or synagogue?

Churched	yes	100%		
Unchurched	yes	26%	no	74%

When looking at the habits of a prayer life, some evidence starts to illuminate the larger picture of the living style and social expressions of both groups. Eighty-nine percent of the churched group say that they pray privately—close to that is the 84 percent of the unchurched. But now catch the difference: Another 66 percent of the churched also state that they pray during a worship service—not so for the unchurched; for they are not in regular attendance, so only 19 percent answer affirmatively here. The incidence of "shared prayer" begins to slide even lower when we poll prayer in the home with other members of the family, at mealtimes, and with other groups (but not during services). Some 44 percent of the churched have a prayer or blessing before meals—only 21 percent of the unchurched. Another 21 percent of the churched are part of group prayer experiences away from home or church—only 8 percent of the unchurched have that sort of social/religious experience with others. The unchurched have, indeed, a faith without fellowship, praying is done alone. A vast number of Christ's followers are without faces or names, or generally accepted identification.

Alienating Forces

When we recognize the mobility of the American population, we are looking at one of the primary opponents of regular church attendance and membership. To move is to become dislocated from the primary systems of social and religious life which once were important to a person or family. The upsetting disarray brought by geographic shifts for individuals and households is influencing the churched as well as the unchurched. Indeed, a significant proportion (one in four) of the churched who are presently active said there was a period of two years or more when they were among the ranks of the unchurched, that is, they did not attend a church or synagogue. When the survey probed these respondents for the reasons for their absence, they were most likely to say,

"I moved to a different community and never got involved in a new church."

or—

"I found other interests and activities which led me to spend less and less time on church-related activities."

On the other hand, the unchurched person who acknowledged being two years or more from church attendance was most likely to say,

"When I grew up and started making decisions of my own, I stopped going to church."

In one sense, we have three different groups within this massive survey of the spiritual climate of America: *the churched, the unchurched, and the rechurched.*

The moving, shifting sensations that motivate men and women to recapture their religious expressions within religious insitutions are highlighted in four categories—four factors or spiritual promptings seem to take place:

1. Self-need
2. Desire for children to have religious instruction
3. A matter of faith
4. A personal religious experience.

Just as these are the positive four, pushing, nudging, prompting, church involvement, so there are another four working against the institutional church:

1. Sports, recreational activity, and hobbies
2. Social activities with friends
3. A work schedule that makes church attendance difficult
4. The desire for "more time for myself and/or family."

These last four interests, however, were not as frequently mentioned as negative effects as the chief reason given by 42 percent of the people who moved to a new community and never became reaffiliated to a church or synagogue. This large group said simply that "seeking a new church was not a matter of urgency, and I never got around to it." While the unchurched mentioned "never getting around to it" in high percentages, the reason cited next most frequently (by 14 percent) was "none of the churches near my home was to my liking." That was followed by 10 percent who said that there "were no churches of my preferred denomination at a convenient distance from my new home."

Less church involvement finally settled down into the categories below—some of which the Christian community can respond to, while others are really out of its control (such as work schedules, illness, or some forms of disability). Most frequently cited were:

- competing activities
- objections to the church's teachings or members
- making one's own decisions
- moving to a different community

- belief that the church was no longer helping in a search for life's meaning or purpose
- a different life-style

Another category of opposition by the churched came from those who said they had problems with the church which contributed to their reduced involvement and attendance:

- teachings about beliefs
  were too narrow   37 percent
- too much concern for money   32 percent
- moral teachings too narrow   28 percent
- dislike traditional forms of worship   23 percent

At least one person in five said, "I wanted deeper spiritual meaning than I found in the church or synagogue."

The concern or regret that the unchurched have over "narrowness" may refer to a variety of beliefs and practices. The objection may be to belief in the inerrancy of scripture. Or, an individual's experience in very conservative congregations may lead that person to believe that all Christian bodies invariably are "narrow." "Narrowness" may be interpreted in such practices as strict dress codes; opposition to social dancing, use of alcoholic beverages—sometimes even cola and coffee—and all kinds of smoking; censure of profanity, participation in public amusement—especially motion pictures and legitimate theater; very restrained, subdued public worship—without music, liturgical robes, and stained-glass windows. This kind of religious world is presently rejected by many within the ranks of the unchurched.

Others may well describe the narrowness of the

church in terms of its moral and ethical teachings. The call for restraint and self-control in matters of sexual behavior and alcohol and drug use, in particular, are considered offensive by many among the un-churched. In these two specific areas we have confirmed evidence that the unchurched are twice as interested—would "welcome" wider acceptance of sexual freedom and more acceptance of marijuana usage. Only 19 percent of the churched would "welcome" acceptance of sexual freedom, while the unchurched are no less than 37 percent behind such a trend. Likewise the churched are only 12 percent positive toward acceptance of marijuana, while the unchurched come in at 28 percent.

The restraint, narrowness, and concern of the church in these matters is not about to go away; indeed, it may actually be increasing its standards and ethical expectations. The unchurched person who enters most Christian fellowships now will be expected to alter his or her attitudes and practices, rather than the other way around.

The priorities of a secular society are going to be in constant tension with the goals and expectations of the Christian community, and the people outside the church are going to experience the conflict and stress that comes from trying to reconcile the two. Today's outsiders, the unchurched, the "unpresent," resent appeals for money—so said 32 percent, almost a third—and part of their complaint may be justified. Congregations and religious fellowships can spend a lot of cash on marginal projects with secondary Christian values at stake. A newer carpet, nicer drapes, a better bell tower does not seem to have a life or death imperative about it. Pleas for parochial education Sunday after Sunday can be tiring, creating a turn-off, shut-out sensation in the impatient worshiper. The steady litany about selling tickets, producing dollars from car washes, bake sales, rummage sales, fashion shows, tickets for auctions, dances, bazaars, raffles, or whatever, can, at last, be just too much for even the most faithful. However, that really is something that every Christian community can change and redesign rather swiftly—from selling to meaningful stewardship; from promoting to the true teaching of tithing and proportionate giving. Yet when the change does happen, there will still remain many among the 32 percent who resent talk about money, for they have made their dollar commitments to the indulgences of the secular kingdom, its allure of sports, recreation, social investment, and travel expectations that add up to thousands of dollars of income and set aside very little, if anything, for charity. What they finally resent is a commitment beyond their own selfish desires. Henry Fairlie, writing about the sin of sloth, notes that it infects millions of people today for it is a state of mind, feeling, and spirit that prevents one from pursuing what is meaningful and good in life. He argues that

> our popular speech is today full of phrases that suggest an indifference and apathy that amount to spiritual and emotional torpor. Hang loose! Laid back! I can dig that, man! Play it cool! Go with the flow! That's heavy! Don't get uptight! There is Sloth in all of them, and they have

their counterpart in more traditional phrases. I couldn't care less! I don't give a damn! What's that to me! I mind my own business! Live and let live! Nothing is worth getting very serious about, except one's own immediate environment. I'm O.K., you're O.K. So what reason is there to worry?

"In the world it is called Tolerance, but in hell it is called Despair," says Dorothy Sayers. It is the sin that believes in nothing, cares for nothing, lives for nothing, and remains alive because there is nothing for which it will die. As each generation in the modern age has followed deeper in the footprints of its predecessors, this description applied to it with continually more accuracy and force. There is not a trumpet note in our lives to call us to our feet.[8]

The constant and heaviest percentage of responses from the unchurched is the report that great chunks of time and energy and affection are being spent on "sports, recreational activities, and hobbies"—some 38 percent are into such pursuits—which prevent them from gaining a meaningful or lasting involvement with a church. Many would argue that their new religion of sports and recreation, back-packing and tennis, has brought them into new heights of spirituality and faith. Says Jim Fixx, the author of the runners' bestseller:

Running has nothing, absolutely nothing to do with caring about other people or with compassion or with self-sacrifice . . . it need hardly be pointed out that self-sufficiency (which running confirms) is the opposite to the human community that is at the heart of the

---

[8]*The Seven Deadly Sins Today* (University of Notre Dame Press, 1978), p. 114.

religious impulse . . . It is a mistake to confuse cardiovascular fitness with *caritas*. . . . A sweat suit is not a surplice. Gatorade is not communion wine.[9]

Yet it is possibly one of the sly temptations that beset modern man that he should believe that his motorcycle or skateboard or hot tub or racquet court will bring him the great experience of the soul.

Again, British social commentator and theologian Henry Fairlie sees the malaise of Western culture in its lunge after sports fads as a valued substitute for the feeding of the inner person:

> The recent popularity of outdoor sports—on the tennis court or the golf course, carrying surfboards to the sea and then carrying them back again, marathon running or even just jogging, and a score more that are now pursued with zealotry—is evidence of a society whose members imagine that they are being strenuous when they are only engaging in a whiffling activity of the body. There is nothing against such activities in themselves. There is everything against the celebration of them as some kind of strenuous spirituality.

> When runners or joggers say that they experience a "high"—a characteristic word of our time—they are talking precisely about a whiffling sensation. A high is whiffling by nature, to be enjoyed as such if that is one's taste, but hardly to be regarded as an encounter with truth. To improve one's tennis is to improve one's tennis. It is not to improve one's soul, even if one has called Zen to one's aid.[10]

---

[9]"What Running Can't Do for You," *Newsweek* (December 18, 1978), 21.

[10]*Seven Deadly Sins*, pp. 121-22.

*Where the Unchurched
and the Churched Meet*

Areas of Common Concern and Agreement

The extensive study of the unchurched (the largest ever attempted in the history of polling) revealed that a large reservoir of goodwill and positive feelings reside in the hearts of a majority of those who were self-designated as unchurched. The unchurched respondents said by 52 percent that they could foresee the possibility of a situation in the future where they might "become a fairly active member" of a church or synagogue. Indeed, of that group, 16 percent said "definitely yes" and another 11 percent, "probably yes," when asked whether they could envision a future activity and involvement with the church.

Where will those developments come from and what are the conditions which seem most favorable at this reading?

1. Some 32 percent said they would be back in the Christian fellowship if they could find a pastor or church friends with whom they could easily and openly discuss their religious doubts. This is a fair and necessary expectation—it relates to the anxiety that many of the unchurched have about the "narrowness" or strictness of a particular theological stance or style of faith expression.

   This group also said that they would like to openly discuss their "spiritual needs" with a church leader or congregational member—here again is a hesitant, tentative plea for a spiritual pilgrimage. The hunger of the soul is deep and personal. One rarely can probe the yearnings of the heart and soul with casual acquaintances or routine business associates. This dialogue of the spirit must be gentle, trusting, and positive. When people—lay or ordained—become known for such personal ministries, the inquirers find them.

2. Some 14 percent of the unchurched were emphatic about finding a church that not only had good preaching but also is "seriously concerned to work for a better society." Close to this was an interest in a religious organization that had a "good program or religious education for children and youth."

This is one of the great common goals of all people—to improve their society and to strengthen the lives of children and youth in the powerful ways of mental and spiritual development.

If the churches are to be authentic and society healthy and whole, a vigorous response is needed to the ethical decay which has so extensively touched all areas of national life. Gilbert Highet, a profound and influential scholar at Columbia University, suggested the challenge that faces us in our present social scene:

> Most people are not irresponsible. Most people have more to lose than to gain by anti-social actions: property, a job, marriage and children, the thought of illness and age, the fear of disgrace restrain them.
>
> But many young men and some girls between fifteen and twenty-five are temporarily or permanently rebels. To win them over and to use their talents for their own

benefit and ours, we must calm them down, divert their energies into harmless channels, commend regularity and diminish harmful excitement. Such excitement is most dangerous in three areas: sex, violence, and intoxication.[11]

The unchurched are saying, by almost 75 percent, that they want their children to have religious instruction and the exposure to Christian teaching and an ethical world-view. People by the millions are concerned, interested—and even desperate—for moral balance and strength in their lives. The Judeo-Christian ethical perspective is the foundation of American institutional life as well as most personal convictions. The Ten Commandments and the commandments of responsible love and justice form the structure of the Bible. While other agencies, organizations, and institutions may *reflect* this stance in Western culture, the church is the source, through the Bible, tradition, and the conviction of its adherents. A belief in God and a pursuit of the moral dimensions seen and interpreted in God's will is the ultimate strength of any religious society that is practicing its faith.

The advertisements, promotions, and inducements of a drug culture are being firmly resisted by the church. There is new evidence that indicates that the church is prepared to take even stronger stands against alcohol abuse and drug addiction (i.e., marijuana smoking and inhalation of cocaine).

An age that has gotten wealthy on sex, violence, and

---

[11]*Man's Unconquerable Mind* (New York: Columbia University Press, 1954), p. 83.

intoxication is going to be in constant warfare with the teachings and practices of the Christian community. On the other hand, people burned-out and disgusted with the returns from a life of sex, violence, and intoxication will look more and more to a bona fide religious community for deliverance. Those seeking a preventive stance against these ills will more and more endorse and advocate the programs and persuasions of the church. Dr. Highet argues that

> In a few important areas of life, description easily passes over into persuasion; the excitement of knowing about certain experiences soon stimulates the emotions so strongly that the entire personality may easily be altered unless it has been carefully prepared, by moral and intellectual training, to resist.
>
> St. Augustine describes how a friend of his went under protest to the greatest of Roman festivals, the games. The young man closed his eyes, in order not to see the gladiators butchering one another, the swords flashing, the blood spouting, the fall of the wounded, the triumph of the victors, and the final moment when the broad, sharp blade plunged into the living flesh. But he heard the yell of excitement from the crowd around him: he opened his eyes; and in a moment he was captured, enjoying the blood and savagery, roaring with delight at the next murder.[12]

Whether we consider Rome then or Rome now, there is the same urgency for people to gather up and integrate within their personality the "moral and

---

[12]*Ibid.*, p. 86.

intellectual training to resist." Without question there have been times and seasons when the Christian community seemed to be the last to recognize the need for meaningful sex education for its families and youth. Conservative Christians, both Catholics and Protestants, have argued against valuable and necessary education in the matter of biology, birth control, family planning, and personal sexual counseling. Fortunately this attitude of mindless resistance has not prevailed, for a healthy yet morally responsible ethic has been the majority position of the Christian community today. As Professor Highet observes,

> Most people find their most constant happiness lies in enjoying a normal sexual relationship, prepared for through their adolescence, and extending into their love for their children. But during youth, nearly everyone is tempted to commit acts and acquire habits which are by general consent, degrading or foolish.
> *One of the purposes of group discipline, in the family, in the church, school, college, and society generally, is to help young people to pass through that period without too much disturbance at the time and remorse and misery later* (italics added).[13]

Alas, there is a lot of remorse and misery out there; many lives fractured by degrading and foolish adventures. The churches and the unchurched have both been there—and both must know where to reach for the answer: "Ask, and it will be given you; seek, and

---

[13]*Ibid.*, p. 85.

you will find; knock, and it will be opened to you," so Jesus is quoted in Matthew 7:7.

Religious Training

All of our studies indicate that the unchurched American has had a traditional religious background—in fact, almost identical to that of the churched! About nine in ten (88 percent) of the churched received religious training of some sort as children, compared to 77 percent of the unchurched. The sharpest difference appears in the *kind* of religious training that was experienced during childhood, for both groups report almost identical involvement with Sunday school as children—76 percent for the churched and 77 percent for unchurched. But when we come to instruction in the home, the gap widens. Among the unchurched, 33 percent reported receiving religious training in the home, while the churched stated that 46 percent had been trained in spiritual matters at home. Parental influence and the training or nontraining by parents comes through in many different ways. For instance, the unchurched respondents noted that the church attendance of their mothers was frequent for some 49 percent, and occasional for about 20 percent. The church group really soars with 73 percent—a broad gap of 24 percent—saying their mother frequently attended church. We also note the same gap in parental church-going when studying the practice of fathers and attendance at worship services. Churched people said that their fathers were in "frequent" attendance by some 55 percent, for the unchurched group, the attendance level slides to 31 percent. Again, interestingly, there is a 24 percent gap between the groups we are studying.

Parental influence through religious home training and the example of fathers and mothers themselves in church attendance seems to be the most powerful difference in the life pattern of respondents—both positively and negatively—if early childhood training is taken *by itself*. For when we examine the other sources of statistical data, we discover that unchurched people who went to Sunday school "every week" as children did so by some 59 percent—a higher percentage of attendance than that of their parents—revealing that these youngsters were sent rather than *always* being accompanied by their parents.

Of the unchurched who went on to receive special training for church membership or who belonged and attended a confirmation class as youths, attendance patterns were almost identical as those for the churched during those early years. Some went for six months, some six months to a year, some for more than a year. So we sense that, at present, lengthy and persistent teaching does not in itself guarantee involvement or membership in adult life. Other forces are operative, powerfully so, and we look to them now.

The people who went on from the combination of religious training in the home and attendance at church school to become members of a congregation said they joined a particular religious fellowship because they were brought up in that congregation. Nearly half the responses fall into this category. A wide variety of influences have been noted, but in summary the factors that most often lead to a youngster becoming an active church member are these:

Father attends church regularly
Mother attends church regularly
Young person attends church school every week
Young person attends communicants' or confirmation class
The person's family does not move around a lot

Reasons churched people are drawn to a particular religious group currently include: friends, good preaching, a good program of religious education. Most significantly, one of the big reasons is simply, "I was invited to the church by a member, and I liked the people."

Blueprints of a Future Church- More Women, Youth, and Television

The leadership of women in the church will continue, with more and more gaining ordination. Surveys of youth, i.e., the Dayton study, present fascinating clues as to where young adults project their future church involvement will be. The electric church is part of the future of faith, with negative and positive effects. And all these features will be wrapped around with music.

The Role of Women

The acceptance of women for ordination within the Christian community is a growing reality that even the most conservative elements are finding hard to resist. We have noted the steady decline of hardcore opposition within the U.S. Roman Catholic Church—a decline of 10 percent from 1974 to 1977. Also, during this time frame, the Episcopal Church voted to ordain women to the office of clergy, a significant step when one considers the cautiousness of the Anglican tradition and the risks to its long-time connections with the Orthodox churches. For many years both the Orthodox and the Roman Catholic communions have looked upon the Anglicans as the "bridge church" to world Protestantism, with Roman Catholics especially alert to the role Anglicans played in interpreting the "catholic experience."

Peter Day, writing in *Ecumenical Trends* admitted that the

> decision of the Episcopal Church to permit the ordination of women to the priesthood has led to a cooling of relationships with the Orthodox Churches. Although women had been made deacons in the early days of the [Orthodox] church, they have not been made deacons in more recent times and have never been ordained to the priesthood in the entire history of Orthodoxy. For generations the Anglican Communion and the Episcopal Church have been welcome friends of the Orthodox Churches and have often found themselves in agreement with Eastern answers to questions still argued in the West . . . the seamless robe of Orthodox tradition apparently does not find room for innovation, however.[1]

Reforms, advances, and innovations within the churches are not without price—and the cost to these historic friends is painful and sad. Yet the movement

---

[1]"The National Ecumenical Consultation of The Episcopal Church," 8 (May 1979), p. 77.

by women for more and more recognition and leadership in the wider Christian community is as old as the New Testament. The promise of God that his Son would appear on earth was made to a believing woman, Mary. "And the angel said to her, 'Do not be afraid, Mary, for you have found favor with God' " is the introduction offered in Luke 1:30. As we trace the ministry of Jesus, we see that women play a vital sustaining role in it. Our Lord is given hospitality and support by women; they are the ones who stay with him all the way to the foot of the Cross; on Easter morning it is Mary Magdalene and Joanna and Mary, the mother of James, who first know of his resurrection and rush to inform the disciples (see Luke 24:9).

And when the Risen Lord urges his followers to remain in Jerusalem until "you shall be baptized with the Holy Spirit," the faithful return to the fellowship of the upper room. Here the disciples regroup, elect a successor for Judas, and examine anew the prophecies of Scripture. And in preparation for the receiving of the Holy Spirit promised by the Lord, Luke tells us that "All these with one accord devoted themselves to prayer, together *with* the women and Mary the mother of Jesus, and with his brothers" (Acts 1:14).

One cannot put enough emphasis on these words, for a great shift in religious history had taken place— through the life, death, and resurrection of Christ, women had moved with God's leadership from a passive to an active role in the affairs of faith and practice. Not only were women no longer subordinate as defined by Jewish law (as well as Gentile practice), they were to become the sponsors of the young church as it moved through Asia Minor and around the rim of the Mediterranean. Churches were organized in homes. And when Paul wants to remind his star protégé, Timothy, of his powerful Christian heritage and urge him to gather a fresh perspective on his ministry, he says, "I am reminded of your sincere faith, a faith that dwelt first in your grandmother Lois and your mother Eunice and now, I am sure, dwells in you" (2 Timothy 1:5).

From New Testament times to the present, the role of women has been essential to the growth and expansion of global Christianity. In recent Gallup studies, we see the leadership of women in secular assignments to be on the increase. In fact, one of the most dramatic trends in public opinion in the Gallup Poll's forty-one-year history is the phenomenal growth in the percent of Americans who say they would have no objection to voting for a woman for President of the United States. In 1937 only one person in three (31 percent) would accept the presidential candidacy of a female; today that figure is 73 percent! Another survey result shows that seven in ten Americans believe the nation would be governed as well, or better, if more women held political office.

It could be argued that women have earned a formal, official role in our churches, since over the years women, on an informal basis in many congregations, have been the backbone of organized religion in America. All of our studies, surveys, and polls support this fact: women are more religious than men, hold their beliefs more firmly, practice their faith more consistently, and work more vigorously for the church.

It is not illogical to conclude that if women in any given church were to lose interest or become disheartened and drop out, that particular church would not only lose its vitality but be in real danger of losing its future.

By large majorities, women not only make up the bulk of membership in the churches of America but by far attend in the greatest numbers. They have the highest confidence in the institutional church, hold religious beliefs to be "very important," and believe, against other trends and attitudes of our society, that "religion as a whole is increasing its influence on American life." If that notion, or belief, continues in North America, it very well may be that the women in the Christian church have been largely responsible for its success.

It is interesting to note that the two Christian bodies resisting the ordination of women, the Orthodox and the Catholic, have continued to have the highest percentage of women in attendance during an average week of any of the denominations—58 percent female versus 51 percent male in the Catholic church and in the Orthodox, a staggering 71 percent female to 29 percent male.

The society in which we live is dependent on the volunteer efforts of its members, and we note in our surveys that women are the backbone of volunteer activities. Statistics reveal that women from educated backgrounds, 30 years and older, living in the South and West, residing in cities of a half million or more, married, and who consider themselves to be evangelically inclined lead the way in charity and social service. When this information is linked to our surveys which state that some 40 million adults consider themselves to be evangelical, and since this group is the fastest growing in the United States, we feel confident in expecting a new surge for the Christian community—in growth, in social and civic improvement, and in a return to the values of home, marriage, and public responsibility.

Perhaps the prophecy of Thomas Wolfe is now coming to pass.

> I believe that we are lost in America, but I believe we shall be found. . . . I think the life we have fashioned in America, and which has fashioned us—the forms we have made, the cells that grew, the honeycomb that was created—was self-destructive in nature and must be destroyed. I think these forms are dying and must die, just as I know that America and the people in it are deathless, undiscovered, and immortal and must live.

Outreach to Youth

The future of the church will rise or fall on its success with young people, and a continuing flow of information tells us that the following characteristics are prominent among American youth:

—A strong desire to live a good life and an awareness of the need to grow spiritually

—Sensitivity to injustice and concern over trends toward immorality in society

—Eagerness for change and innovation—true characteristics of youth

—Interest in a life of service—nearly one-third of the

respondents of the Dayton survey said they would like to go into some kind of social outreach as their life's work

—Influence of religious faith in terms of providing guidance, comfort, and inspiration as well as providing restraint and self-control in personal conduct. For example, a large percent of youth in the Dayton comprehensive survey said that their religion helped them control their tempers and restrain hostile feelings. Others said that their thoughts about God and their religious training helped them to resist temptation, such as robbing from a store or smashing a window. Other young adults said that their religion and its leadings made them kinder and more loving, while another group concluded that their devotion to God and their faith gave them courage when they faced crises.

In our studies of overseas young people in eleven different nations, studies sponsored by the Japanese government in which Gallup International conducted more than 15,000 in-person interviews with youths between the ages of 18–24, we found American youth, next to Filipino youths, to be the best churchgoers. American youth are not only exceptionally religious when compared to those from other nations (74 percent of the youth of Japan say they have no interest in religion), but also put a higher premium on "love and sincerity" as a goal in life and less on "money and position."

American youth also appear to be more outgoing— more eager to lend a helping hand to someone in need—than were the youth of other nations, with the exception of youth in Switzerland, that is, if such a conclusion can be drawn from a single question. Youth in the United States and Switzerland were more inclined to say that if they were to meet a man lost and trying to find his way, they would ask him if he needed help. In contrast, youth in the other nine nations leaned heavily to the answer, "I would tell him the way if he asked me."

The Electric Church

The advent of the "electronic church" presents an enigma to the future of institutional religion as well as the vitality of the Christian faith. First of all, people watch a lot of television, and our young people have never known a day without it. The Dayton Study confirms the importance of television in the lives of the latest generation on their way to adulthood: The majority of young people state that it is one of their favorite ways to spend an evening. A large group (56 percent) watches television for more than two and one-half hours every day. Apparently this could be a great potential medium for churches in reaching the outsider as well as the backslider, young or old.

In his pacesetting article on the electric church published in the *Wall Street Journal* of May 19, 1978, Jim Montgomery revealed the sharp truth that radio and television religious personalities had created a brand new church—one that may well be draining the effectiveness of local congregations all over the Western hemisphere. Writes Montgomery,

The Electric Church is a booming industry generating thousands of jobs and an annual cash flow of hundreds of millions of dollars. . . . According to Prof. Martin Marty, the big broadcast ministries are in effect becoming a new church. Noting, for instance, that the national headquarters of most major established denominations each receive $20 million to $30 million a year from local congregations, he adds, "Any self-respecting evangelist can do better than that on TV."

The article noted that there are at least eight superstars who gather a quarter of a billion dollars a year through their multimedia fundraising. Jerry Falwell, pastor of the Thomas Road Baptist Church in Lynchburg, Virginia, believes that his Old Time Gospel Hour may soon be pulling a million dollars a week. Oral Roberts' ministry is running close to $60 million a year and growing at "an annual rate of 25% to 30%." In Pasadena, California, the father-and-son team of Herbert W. and Garner Ted Armstrong was bringing in about $75 million annually. When we look at the fairly recent entry of religion into the telecommunications field, Pat Robertson and the 700 Club come to mind. So does Jim Bakker (pronounced "Baker"), who started the successfully syndicated show called The PTL Club. Surprisingly, the oldest and most famous, The Billy Graham Evangelistic Association, receives about $30 million a year—far down the list of receipts when compared to the other electronic ministries. This is especially ironic because Graham's crusades are more closely linked to local churches than the above-mentioned personalities. Rex Humbard, broadcasting from Canton, Ohio, and Robert Schuller,

famous for a very successful drive-in church ministry in
Orange County, California, round out the personalities regularly seen on television who are enjoying an
amazing response through mail and contributions and
viewing.

Needless to say, the success and stunning monetary
growth of the electric church has been considered a
mixed blessing by the main-line churches in North
America. Most active parish Christians would salute
the efforts of any who brings the message and invitation
of Jesus Christ to a secular, indifferent, and often
unreachable audience out there in television land.
Encouragement through prayer, Bible study, praise
and worship, and financial giving are all basic to the
development and enhancement of the Christian life.
Yet the electric church appears to be in competition
with the corner congregation, and with the exception of
the Graham ministry which faithfully links its message
to that of neighborhood churches, is satisfied to do just
that.

Martin E. Marty, church historian and Lutheran
pastor in Riverside, Illinois, portrays the familiar scene
rather vividly:

> Late Saturday night Mr. and Mrs. Invisible Religion get
> their jollies from the ruffled-shirted, pink-tuxedoed
> men and the high-coiffured, low-necklined celebrity
> women who talk about themselves under the guise of
> Born Again autobiographies. Sunday morning the
> watchers get their jollies as Holy Ghost entertainers
> caress microphones among spurting fountains and a
> highly professional charismatic (in two senses) leader
> entertains them. Are they to turn off that very set and

then make their way down the block to a congregation
of real believers, sinners, offkey choirs, and sweaty and
homely people who need them, people they do not like
but are supposed to love, ordinary pastors who preach
grace along with calls to discipleship, pleas for
stewardship that do not come well-oiled? Never. Well,
hardly ever.[2]

Without question, the surprising success of religious
television is forcing the main-line churches to reexamine
their stance toward the medium and to explore new ·
strategies that reflect the goals and style of their
membership. In the spring of 1979, the Roman Catholic
Church announced a $7 million fund to be established
for the advancement of the church's message on radio,
television, and in print media. Headed by Bishop Joseph
R. Crowley, the prelates of America set aside World
Communications Day to receive an offering across the
nation. A vast group of 240 church communication
specialists plus another 60 experts from publishing,
radio, and television broadcasting, film producers and
advertising executives will be used to direct the main
thrust of the telecommunications enterprise.

Other Christian denominations have been studying
their entry or reentry into the media marketplace.
The United Presbyterian Church will soon receive
recommendations from its own task force as to what
techniques, programs, and content it should pursue in
regard to the public proclamation of the Gospel.
Archbishop Fulton J. Sheen, the leading religious

---

[2]"The Electronic Church," *Missouri in Perspective* (March 27,
1978), 5.

broadcaster in the eyes of many Catholics, and not a few Protestants, said the new effort of his own church was "to reach not only those who belong to the faith but all the unchurched and all the souls in America who are consciously or unconsciously searching for God."

Recent surveys conducted nationally by the United Presbyterian Church demonstrate the far-reaching effects of the mass media on the opinions and spiritual growth of individual members. More than a third of the members polled stated that television evangelists and preachers were "very important" or "somewhat important" in the formulation of their opinions regarding controversial questions, such as the Christian stance on abortion or homosexuality.

When the same group was asked if radio and television evangelists had advanced their growth as a Christian through their preaching, a majority of 56 percent said that Billy Graham "to a great extent or to some extent" had exerted such an influence. The other leading personality was Oral Roberts—some 35 percent saying that he had influenced them to "a great extent or to some extent."

What was most revealing about the Presbyterian survey, concerning the personal life of individual church members and the sources they regularly turned to for growth and guidance as a Christian, was the high percentage of persons who said the influence of their local pastor or discussions with persons they respected was helpful. In fact, 86 percent said that their pastor's preaching was the most helpful resource for personal Christian growth. The same group said that discussion with a "respected person" for guidance was a significant growth aid in their faith—some 76 percent in this majority.

In the same checklist, a majority of 52 percent identified small study or Bible study groups as providing the support system for their faith. Interestingly, the lowest source mentioned as an aid to Christian growth was television and radio programs—only 23 percent listed this as a force in the process of spiritual development.

The Presbyterian Panel (the name of the Presbyterian national membership survey) touched on habits of prayer, religious reading habits, and devotional practices, as well as what hymns, scriptures, and prayers were most favored. When asked to name the moment when they felt most a sense of being at worship with God, 80–95 percent of all surveyed said it was during the celebration of the Lord's Supper.

At this point in our discussion, it is clearly apparent that the returns and rewards of the Christian life for persons active in their congregations come from the sharing and seeking of God's word. Consequently, the power of the pulpit in shaping and encouraging Christian growth is without threat from any other source, and the partaking of the Lord's Supper remains one of the high and holy moments in the life of a Christian. One feels close to God and to those sharing the experience, and that is a vivid, confirming sign of a true and living faith.

This is not to say that telecommunications will not be a powerful voice—or picture—in shaping the future design of the Christian experience. Yet the present program arrangement of the electric church presents only one aspect of the Christian life, and if this were the only exposure for a potential communicant, it would be distorted and weird, indeed.

In his commentary on American pluralism in a chapter of *Religion in America,* Martin Marty elaborates on the complexity of the current spiritual upheaval and expands on the "invisible church," a term coined by sociologist Thomas Luckmann.

> He [Luckmann] refers to the fact that in a consumer society that assures great freedom, including the freedom to be nonreligious or utterly selective, many people find meaning without belonging, religion without community.

> They pick and choose among the offerings of the bookstore, the television set, the magazine rack, the dormitory, and the promptings of the heart. They are free to be eclectic, taking this from science and that from Zen, this from remembered Catholicism and that from hoped-for therapy, to form what Margaret Mead in one speech called "a mishmash of all the religions ever known."

Martin then gets down to the heart of our present situation in the latter part of the twentieth century:

> The invisible religion is invisible because it is private, personal, not regularly institutionalized, not monitored by priests or contained in organizations. As such it lacks specific social power. Nowhere can it be mapped. But personal religion is chosen by millions as an alternative to religionlessness or godlessness. They must be getting something out of it.

If millions of people are attracted, there must be some impact even if they are not organized as a force. . . . This religion of "the highrise apartment and the long weekend" is likely to grow and be an ever more confusing alternative to church membership than anti-religion or mere secularity ever was.[3]

When we consider the church of the future and its future on television—which has all the grand ingredients of a classic love/hate relationship—we want to remind ourselves that Christians are the people of the Book. A key New Testament book starts off by saying "In the beginning was the Word, and the Word was with God, and the Word was God." The Gospel writer, John, took the Greek word *logos* and found in it all the promises and powers of God, for he soon added, "And the Word became flesh and dwelt among us, full of grace and truth; we have beheld his glory, glory as of the only Son from the Father" (v. 14). So not only is the Word primary and essential to the believing Christian community, but so also is the Word of God revealed as it is understood and affirmed by reading and studying its proclamation in the Scriptures.

Christians have always claimed that the prayerful and careful study of God's Word as revealed through the Testaments was imperative for an understanding faith in Christ—and more, that the Holy Spirit is given as part of that study, prayerful, perceiving process. While Christians carry different interpretations about the holiness of particular words, phrases, and sentences, there is little

---

[3] *Religion in America*, p. 83.

doubt that true believers feel led to the will of God through and by his word.

It simply is not possible nor desirable for Christians to accept tapes, films, videotaped broadcasts, or cassettes as a viable and lasting substitute for the individual or group encounter with the Word of God as revealed through the pages of the Bible. This is a vital personal encounter and one to which Christians keep coming back as the source and inspiration of their faith.

In a national Presbyterian poll, adult members stated that they considered the Bible to be a very important or somewhat important guide in formulating their opinions on controversial questions by an 85 percent majority; pastors responding to the same inquiry looked to the Bible by a 98 percent majority.[4] The pursuit of biblical studies on the seminary, graduate school level is on a steady increase as are the Bible study groups active in all branches of the Christian church.

As Christians sort out their response to the puzzling questions regarding the employment and effect of all forms of mass media, it is encouraging to know that a recent Gallup Poll among Catholics shows their concern that they "spend too much time watching television, some 33 percent expressing this television-viewer's guilt complex." Nationwide, television watching may be on the decline, indicating new opportunities for the ancient means of communication, the written word.

---

[4]"Presbyterian Panel," conducted by the Research Division of the Support Agency of the United Presbyterian Church in the U.S.A., August 1978, appendix 10.

Without the Parish the Church May Perish

While many Christian sociologists fear the inroads of the mass media because the media projects the electric church as a pleasant, arm chair substitute for real life Christianity, others believe that the future battles for a meaningful spiritual life will be won or lost in the local parish. The rising anxiety of the main-line denominations over the visiblity and impact of the radio-television evangelists comes from their fear that present mission giving is being syphoned off into independent, unverified "faith projects." Their anxiety may be justified. Rex Humbard has recently sustained a series of court-ordered judgments to refund nonprofit bonds to donors who may not have fully understood their use or security. Convulsions are shaking the Armstrong enterprise in California ("The World Tonight!") where, again, competition among divisions for control of the organization's assets and properties have taken them to court, causing one to wonder about their responsible handling of $60–$70 million a year.

The young people who have run away from the organizational structures of Christianity to follow the gleam of the Maharishi Mahesh Yogi and his casual, relaxed, freed-up, laid-back style of T.M. are in for a few organizational expectations later on. Presently the Maharishi has, according to Henry Fehren, his own Vatican in Switzerland in the guise of an attractive little castle. His corporation now includes "a University in Iowa, and he plans 3,600 World Plan Centers and one teacher for every 1,000 of the World's population."

The cluster of Christians in community is necessary

and timeless. Father Fehren argues that there is no substitute for the parish although "some people think that the parish is about to perish, that it is an outmoded institution, that it is a structure which does not reflect the sense of community we hear so much about today." Many Catholics, he says, want to be free to

> float wherever they please for any sacrament, desert their own parishes and run off to any one which happens to please their cultural, aesthetic, or spiritual palates and have no ties to the parishes in which they live. . . . Two thousand years of experience has taught us that we need the parish. The parish is often the church in miniature and Christ is the heart of each parish.[5]

As Christian people regain their vision of the universal church, they will discover that the local congregation and its surrounding, sustaining parish is where Christ chooses to greet us and sustain us. It is truly impossible to love and honor the Church Universal before we have loved and supported the church in our house, as Saint Paul describes it.

When one considers those tiny, spare upper room congregations all over Asia Minor, carefully planted and watered by the Apostles, one is surely amazed that by the end of the first century there may have been more than a hundred thousand members devoting themselves to prayers, songs, and the breaking of bread. No church colleges, no mountain top retreat centers, no central city cathedrals, and certainly no

---

[5]"Gladly, The Cross-Eyed Bear," *U.S. Catholic* (April 1978), 50-51.

coinage saying, "In God We Trust." The isolated groups of Christians, first in houses and then in house churches, began their inevitable march toward the City of God. Their faith was warm and contagious; they were terribly confident and as Hans Kung has said, they took dead aim on the Roman empire: its slavery, its idolatry, its imperial arrogance, its awesome power. And they won. As Saint Paul would write to the church at Ephesus that it was "through the church the manifold wisdom of God might now be made known to the principalities and powers in the heavenly places" (3:10).

Karl Rahner, the distinguished European theologian, spoke for many when he said:

Let us love the church of weakness.
We are not ashamed of her because there are so many
  shameful things about her.
We must cherish the church as Christ does.
We must fill her with warm love.
We must console her and embrace her.
We must intercede for her with the jealousy of God.
In a word, we must love her in her totality and without
conditions. And behold, precisely in this love, the
transformation of the church from weakness to power,
from crippled ugliness to immortal beauty, is taking
place, silently and irresistibly until the end of time.[6]

Music in the Church's Future

One of the reasons the Christian church will increase its strength and influence in the days and years ahead is

---

[6]*Ibid.*

the power of its music. In the Old Testament, the music of David had the efficacy to calm the troubled soul of King Saul: "David took the lyre and played it with his hand; so Saul was refreshed and was well, and the evil spirit departed." We turn to music in times of trouble, sorrow, and grief; and modern men and women, like ancient believers, can turn no deeper than to the music of the soul. The Christian community is the source and inspiration of that musical experience.

All the celebrations of life worth honoring are circled by song and punctuated by music. So it always has been. When Moses and the people of Israel triumphantly escaped from the clutches of Pharaoh by successfully crossing the Red Sea, the Exodus writings say,

> Then Moses and the people of Israel sang this song
> to the Lord, saying,
>   "I will sing to the Lord, for he has triumphed
>   gloriously;
>   the horse and his rider he has thrown into
>   the sea.
>   The Lord is my strength and my song,
>   and he has become my salvation."
>   Exodus 15:1-2

Can anyone measure the effect and staying power of a single great song bathing the broken lives of struggling people with its grace and hope? Studs Terkel could not. For years he had hosted a popular jazz radio show in Chicagoland. He thought he knew all the talent; he had aired and introduced the highest and the best. Then a friend asked him to listen to a gospel singer on an Apollo label:

It is Gospel. "Move On Up a Little Higher." It builds and builds and builds for six minutes. I am floored and lifted. Who is she? George tells me she lives on the South Side and sings in a lot of black churches. I am caught.[7]

Terkel then starts to visit, on Sundays, the Greater Salem Baptist Church. It's in a flaky neighborhood, for urban renewal has not yet brought the flowers and the lawns. But the gray, bleak world of West Side Chicago becomes incandescent through the singing of Mahalia Jackson. Remembers Terkel:

A single voice, a piano, and an organ. A record label little known. Consider this. More than two million people, way more, have put out hard-gotten cash for "Move On Up a Little Higher." In scores of thousands of homes, among the devout and God-fearing, oh yeah, and in taverns and pool parlors, too. Again and again and again, this record is played on phonographs and jukeboxes. The grooves are worn deep and the needles dulled, but they keep on listening, through scratch and static, to this voice.[8]

In so many respects the Christian community has been slow to recognize this gift that has been given—not only to the sick and tired and beaten and bereaved—but also to the winning, joyful, and recovering who find in song and melody the strength of

[7]*Talking to Myself: A Memoir of My Times* (New York: Pantheon Books, 1973), pp. 260-61.
[8]*Ibid.*

God. Music is the spirit's universal language; it is the vocabulary of the soul, it becomes the chainlink between people when everything else has failed. It is a divine sign that the church has a large future.

D. H. Lawrence, usually expressing unhappy experiences about organized religion, wrote in his poem "Piano,"

> Softly in the dusk, a woman is singing to me;
> Taking me back down the vista of years, till I see
> A child sitting under the piano, in the boom of the
>   tingling strings
> And pressing the small, poised feet of a mother who
>   smiles as she sings.
>
> In spite of myself, the insidious mastery of song
> Betrays me back, till the heart of me weeps to belong
> To the old Sunday evenings at home, with winter
>   outside
> And hymns in the cozy parlour, the tinkling piano
>   our guide.
>
> So now it is vain for the singer to burst into
>   clamour
> With the great black piano appassionato. The glamour
> Of childish days is upon me, my manhood is cast
> Down in the flood of remembrance, I weep like a child
>   for the past.[9]

The uses of music to attract and anchor people within the religious community should not be underestimated.

---

[9]*Complete Poems of D. H. Lawrence,* Vol. 2. Copyright © 1964, 1971, by Angello Ravagli and C. M. Weekley. Reprinted by permission of Viking/Penguin, Inc.

The church is one of the very few places remaining in North America where an individual participates in music as a personal or group expression. Many public school systems have dropped music altogether. Opportunities for children and young people to sing and perform is now almost entirely the province of the church—and a golden opportunity indeed.

The uses of songs and hymns and musicals to convey the message of the soul to the unchurched or unbeliever, as well as to strengthen the spirit of the faithful, cannot be overlooked. On June 10, 1979, the *Denver Post* had this short announcement:

DENVER WILL SING FOR EPISCOPALIANS

Singer John Denver will perform during the national Episcopal convention in Denver this Fall. He will do a benefit program for the church's national hunger committee and proceeds will go to the Presiding Bishop's Fund for World Relief.

Denver will sing September 14 in the Auditorium Theater, concluding a 24 hour period of prayer and fasting by Episcopalions.

Here we see a popular entertainer combining his talent with the concerns of Christians for the hungry, forgotten, and deprived. An outsider would also take note of the twenty-four-hour period of prayer and fasting, one of the most potent forces that Jesus urged his followers to employ when dealing with what seemed to be insurmountable difficulties.

The music of the heart is both universal and timeless. The music of the soul seeks expression and unity with others. The church knows this well, and one of its major strengths heading into the latter part of the twentieth century will be to exploit the grandeur and joy of its music. Carl Sandburg suggested that the life of the prairie gave him a slogan and a song. Longfellow groaned at middle-age that he had not yet built a tower of song. Augustine would reach the deep levels of conversion through the sounds of Christian people singing—and when he did, he discovered that "truth flowed into my heart." Music belongs in the Christian church, and it is ready to caress the world anew with its power.

Religion in America - The Shape of Its Future Already Unfolding

The church of the 80s will be more conservative and frequently orthodox in its theology and ethics. The evangelical tide is rising. A conservative young clergy has arrived, but so has a most powerful sentiment for inter-church, inter-faith relations. Christians like each other and express positive feelings across denominational lines. Will the vitality of the Christian churches be the surprise of the 80s, affecting deeply and positively the wobbling institutions of America?

The Return of an Orthodox Faith

Recent studies demonstrate a powerful return to the conservative tenets of religion. In the instance of Christianity, every survey points to a strong tide running in favor of orthodoxy. This theological stance is reenforced by new Christians who have had a conversion experience and value that moment as one in which Jesus Christ was the central shaper of their lives.

The orthodox position, shared by millions in North America, can be described as a viewpoint that holds that the Bible "as the word of God, is not mistaken in its teachings and statements." The orthodox believer affirms that "Jesus Christ is both fully God and fully man or, more commonly or popularly stated, Jesus Christ was the Son of God." These same believers would go on to state that "the only hope for Heaven is through personal faith in Jesus Christ."

The company of the orthodox is not isolated within a single church or denomination but is found in all branches in Christendom. Orthodox believers, in our polls, state that they "read the Bible at least once a month, attend religious services at least once a month, and have had a religious experience that is still very important in their everyday life." Some 98 percent would say that Jesus Christ was a key factor in that experience and that it was a life-changing moment, a conversion experience.

It is interesting to note the contrasts between the orthodox Christian and the general public in America. While some 69 percent of the general public believe that "God or a universal spirit observes our actions and rewards and punishes you for them," at least 81 percent of the orthodox would agree with that statement. When adults were asked how much consolation and help they gained from their religious beliefs, the general public said by 54 percent that they got a lot of help from such convictions. The orthodox, responding to the same query, said by 89 percent that they received a lot of help from their theology.

As one sifts through the vast amount of data compiled in the past two years concerning the attitudes, beliefs, and convictions of the American public, one discovers that the majority steadily follow or are influenced in the direction of orthodox convictions, no matter what the degree of religious *practice*. The unchurched American may be a puzzle or question or irritating mystery to the religious establishment, but his notions or her theology has a definite tendency to take a conservative/orthodox stance on Christianity. The unchurched stance is difficult to sort out; it may be that inactive Christians are parroting orthodox views because those are the creeds and philosophies they were taught early in life and presently are resisting. Is it possible that men and women who are currently inactive and defined as unchurched propose the "proper" answer in a poll or punch the orthodox response because that was the last one they heard just before they dropped out and decided they had no place to go theologically?

The turmoil within theology in the past decade has not done much to aid the questioning believer or the college-educated student who rejected the literalism of his childhood but found no way into the more mature or sophisticated scholarship of the main-line churches. Indeed, it is possible to argue that the failure of the main-line churches in America properly to interpret the Bible and clarify the scriptures has led thousands not only out of the churches into the ranks of the unchurched but also created prey for the cults which have flourished using a marvelous circus of juggling acts, fire-eating displays, and daredevil exploits all in the name of God as defined by their theology.

When the public at large and orthodox churches were asked the following question about the Bible, both groups, although distant in worship and religious habits, nevertheless seemed to be "tracking" on the same highway of faith. Here is the Bible question:

"Which one of these statements comes closest to describing your feelings about the Bible?

1. The Bible is a collection of writings representing some of the religious philosophies of ancient man.
2. The Bible is the word of God, but it is sometimes mistaken in its statements and teachings.
3. The Bible is the word of God and is *not* mistaken in its statements and teachings."

The literalist believer would accept the third answer as being the truth. That orthodox statement was endorsed by 42 percent of the general public, compared to 100 percent of the orthodox conversionalist groups in the church. (The general public was rather evenly distributed between the first two questions.) While the general public affirms the divinity of Jesus Christ by a strong majority, it also believes, by some 45 percent, that the "only hope for heaven is through personal faith in Jesus Christ." The orthodox would affirm that statement 100 percent.

One of the most surprising findings was that a high percentage of the general public believe in a personal Devil with some 34 percent compared to 70 percent of the orthodoxy holding that belief. Some observers are surprised by this response, suggesting that the mass movies followed by millions, such as *Rosemary's Baby, The Exorcist,* and other exploitation films are emphasizing this particular notion of Christian doctrine.

Even more fascinating is the material uncovered regarding the origin of man. People were asked to pick the statement that came closest to describing their beliefs about Creation:

1. God created Adam and Eve, which was the start of human life.
2. God began an evolutionary cycle for all living things, including man, but personally intervened at a point in time and transformed man into a human being in His own image.

Since the first two statements captured 70 percent of the general public and 94 percent of the orthodox, we could stop right there. But for the sake of comparison, here are the other two:

3. God began an evolutionary cycle for all living things, including man, but did not personally intervene at a point in time and transform man into a human being in His own image.
4. The origin of man is unknown.

The last statement appealed to about 12 percent of the general public and 1 percent of the orthodox Christians. Statement #3 satisfied 11 percent of the public and 3 percent of the orthodox. Statement #2 was chosen by 20 percent of the public and some 9 percent of the orthodox. And for statement #1, mark this; 50 percent of the general public and 85 percent of the orthodox affirm the Genesis story of Adam and Eve as the start of human life on this planet. These high percentages indicate that the debate over evolution versus the creation story of the Old Testament is not resolved.

When we look within the Christian context, certain major groups can be identified as holding the most conservative views in the matter of faith and practice: Catholics, Baptists, and Lutherans. (There is a wide variety of smaller groups that are more conservative than those just mentioned, but they do not involve as large a number of people, e.g., The Church of Christ, The Seventh-Day Adventists, etc.) Belief in the inerrancy of Scripture would be vigorously supported by the *clergy* leadership within the Baptist, Catholic, and Lutheran denominations. For instance, some 70 percent of the Catholic clergy state that the Bible is "the Word of God and is not mistaken in its statements and teachings." Lutheran clergy in America approve that affirmation by some 60 percent, and the Baptists, both Southern and other branches, reach the high water mark of 90 percent.

The contrast with the Methodists, Presbyterians, and Episcopalians is striking, indeed. Methodist clergy state by 47 percent that the Bible is the Word of God, but "sometimes is mistaken in its statements or teachings." In a broader denominational poll which included *both* members and clergy, the following statement was supported by large majorities:

"The Bible is the inspired word of God but not everything in it should be taken literally, word for word."

Episcopal response	61 percent favoring
Presbyterian response	55 percent favoring
Methodist response	47 percent favoring

The reader is aware that polls of the total group are conducted on a regular basis and both clergy and laity included. Other polls are more specific, for example, the canvassing of clergy alone as well as the sampling of specific denominations. The most recent polls of clergy exclusively indicate that younger members of the profession are by far the most conservative, pointing to the conclusion that the orthodox stance in Christianity may be on the rise. Some 78 percent of the younger clergy (ages 18–29) would approve a literalistic interpretation of the Bible compared to 70 percent of their elders (50 and older).

The Conservative Young Clergy— A Cautious Future Faith?

Throughout the current studies regarding the attitudes and convictions of the young clergy of America, a steady conservative image is being revealed. The younger clergy, tomorrow's Christian leaders, believe firmly in the Adam and Eve narrative of Genesis as being the authentic account of the origin of man. Some 70 percent affirm this view compared to 57 percent of the *older* clergy. The young clergy are positive, by 87 percent—the highest tally of any grouping—that Jesus Christ is "the only hope for heaven for those who believe in him." (The Catholic clergy as a total grouping slightly disagree—they say that "heaven is a divine reward for those who earn it in their own good life." This doctrine of works has reigned powerfully through time in the Catholic community and still is operative and persuasive for the clergy of that branch of Christendom. For all the strong signals of ecumenical cooperation and support, this doctrine remains a stumbling block between Protestants and Catholics.)

Of all the clergy age groupings, those in the younger group of 18–29 state they have had a religious experience by higher percentages than the others and, by 93 percent, that it involved Jesus Christ. The great majority of younger clergy said that this was a conversion experience and that it continues to have a sustaining influence in their lives.

The stance and life-style of the younger clergy can be clearly seen in their personal habits, such as their approach to the use of alcoholic beverages. The Catholic clergy overwhelmingly acknowledge the regular use of alcohol—by some 92 percent. The vote of Southern Baptist preachers is just the opposite—a negative 95 percent. Lutherans are Protestants, and possibly as conservative in their theology as the Southern Baptists, except that they are comfortable with an occasional drink by some 94 percent. It should be noted that liturgically the Lutherans and the Roman Catholics celebrate Holy Communion and Mass with wine, while the Baptists use only grape juice. It is intriguing to note that the younger clergy in America, representing all faiths, are also the most negative among the clergy in the rejection of the use of liquor. Some 62 percent of the younger clergy claim to be total abstainers and will probably be teaching and preaching this viewpoint as they move into church and parish leadership. If they have their way, the 1980s will be more dry than wet.

When we consider the clergy attitudes toward divorce, we discover that the large majority of respondents would favor this statement: "Divorce should be avoided except in an extreme situation." However, there were nearly 18 percent of the *young* clergy who opted for a more rigid statement, such as: "Divorce should be avoided under any circumstance."

The Source of Future Authority—The Bible

Extensive studies of clergy attitudes reveal some divergence on the selection of ultimate authority in one's life. Clergy persons were asked to consider a list of possible authorities that they would turn to in sorting out the answers and direction for their faith. They were:

1. By what the church says
2. By what respected religious leaders say
3. By what the Holy Spirit says to me personally
4. By what the Bible says
5. None of these
6. I don't test my religious beliefs.

The Catholic clergy were firm in their trusting of "what the church says" for their final authority (by some 70 percent). The Protestant clergy by almost the identical majority, 76 percent, stated that "what the Bible says" is the trustworthy authority in one's faith. Interestingly, both Protestant and Catholic clergy took the leading of the Holy Spirit as their second choice for direction and guidance in their spiritual questions and pursuit of faith.

The search for trustworthy authority and the resurgence of interest in biblical archaeology points to a high involvement of laity and clergy in Bible study groups in the 80s. Already we have seen interest widening in the Catholic community, and the appearance of new translations throughout the Christian community worldwide indicates that the decade to come will be Bible-centered, indeed.

Feeling Good About the Faith

The phrase "on a scale of one to five"—or one to ten—has been added to the American vocabulary during the last several years. In most Gallup polls a card known as the scalometer is handed to the person being interviewed:

					Don't					
+5	+4	+3	+2	+1	know	−1	−2	−3	−4	−5

The scalometer provides an immediate response device. The individual circles the level of positive or negative feelings toward the topic being discussed knowing that he will not have to defend, argue, or promote his answer at that point.

The scalometer was put to use to find out how people feel about their present religious identification, i.e., how does a person feel, positively or negatively, about his or her church, historic spiritual roots, or present Christian orientation? Consider the following charts:

Chart Reflecting the Self-Esteem of Seven Religious Groups
in America as Seen in Positive Ratings of Membership or
Preference

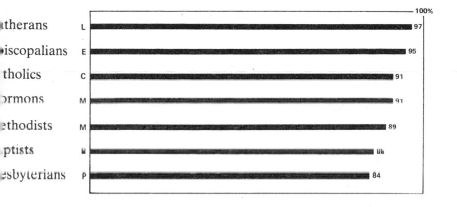

Chart Reflecting the Self-Esteem of Seven Religious Groups
in America When Recording Those Who Indicated <u>5 Plus</u> as
Their Positive Self-Esteem Rating

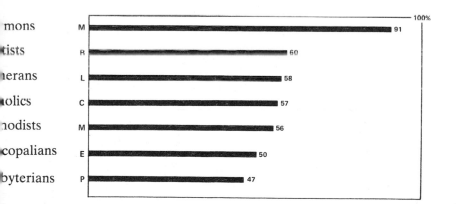

In the category of esteem for one's own religious affiliation, those most positive about their Christian designation are the twelve and a half million Lutherans in America. As a national grouping, they show a 97 percent positive rating on the scalometer. All other religious bodies are lower than this in our findings. The next highest group is the 95 percent self-rating of the Episcopalians. The chart then notes the Roman Catholics at 91 percent. (The Mormons, a non-Christian group, also show a 91 percent self-esteem rating.) Then, in order, follow the Methodists, Baptists, and Presbyterians.

Some editorial reflections should be considered here. In spite of theological commotion, congregational splits, and doctrinal disputes in the Lutheran bodies of America, the individual member remains solid in his faith preference/commitment and responds with an enormous 97 percent vote of loyalty. This highly positive response may be the result of a religious tradition that has always put enormous emphasis on communicant training of youth. It may be that the inherent strength of this branch of Christendom is the astounding Martin Luther who reformed the Christian community in the sixteenth century and helped redirect the course of world history. Lutheran loyalty may be an expression of the power of European ascendants from Germany, the Lowlands, and Scandinavia; and the daily support of language, music, and culture in family, church, and school. However one chooses to interpret these sentiments on the Gallup scalometer, the Lutherans are easily the highest at 97 percent, reflecting a powerful self-identity along with pride in religious affiliation.

The four and a half million Episcopalians feel good about their denominational preference and indicate a loyalty that has carried them through continuing controversies regarding the ordination of women, certain social/political pronouncements, and the revision of their historic *Book of Common Prayer*. The last event brought an explosive and widely felt response. Yet the historic linkage to Canterbury and the trusted structure of church law, liturgy, and world-view is very fulfilling to the members of this great Christian body, strong in the United States and global in its membership. Despite heavy losses in membership between 1966 and 1975—a drop of nearly 17 percent—the Episcopal community in America is not fading away. A 95 percent positive self-image is indicative of a strong body of people.

In spite of the amazing amount of change, stress, upheaval, and controversy that has been traced and discussed earlier in this book, the Catholic community as a whole has one of the highest levels of self-esteem and good feelings about being in the church among the Christian bodies. By 91 percent, members of the Catholic church and people with a Catholic preference, representing some 48 million adults in the United States, express positive and supportive views about their religious persuasion. This is not to ignore the negative voices, however. At least 10 percent of the total Catholic grouping are on the negative side of the meter and a sharp 4 percent show a very negative (minus 5) rating of the whole enterprise. This may reflect two minority groups—the Catholic traditionalist movement made up of those who resent the reforms of Vatican II and consider the changes in the Mass (Latin to English) and the ecumenical overtures of Pope John XXIII as inspired by the Devil, and the most liberal critics, those who want massive and sweeping change in everything from ordination of women to the priesthood, to abortion on demand and the removal of the Swiss guards in the Vatican. Both are small though, at times, visible and vocal groups.

The Methodists—some sixteen and a half million adults who claim a preference for the church of John Wesley—have a positive esteem level of 89 percent, followed by some 31 million Baptists who arrive at an 85 percent figure on the scalometer. These somewhat lower self-ratings should be judged in light of the fact that the groups tallied are much larger than the first two and more diverse culturally than the Lutheran and Episcopal communities.

The Presbyterians are a puzzle—if not to others, at least to themselves. Compared to others, they have the lowest self-esteem rating on the charts, recorded at 84 percent positive regarding membership and 47 percent positive on the question of self-esteem. Some reasons or causes are obvious. Controversial pronouncements emanating from their annual Assemblies, the Civil Rights movement, and other social action issues put the followers of John Calvin and John Knox in the middle of the sixties' tumult. Long-term commitments to the issues of war and peace, minority rights, women's awareness, followed by a drastic and, some would say, damaging restructuring of denominational life from top to bottom further weakened or disabled the Presbyterians—at least the majority group (there are about a dozen different Presbyterian or Reformed churches in the United States), The United Presbyterian Church in the United States of America. The Presbyterians lost millions of members in the seventies, apparently as a result of the tensions within the church brought on by these social issues and church restructuring.

Cooperation and Conflict
Among the Christian Churches

It is now two decades since Bishop James Pike of the Episcopal Church and Dr. Eugene Carson Blake of the United Presbyterian Church proposed a sweeping merger among four Christian denominations in North America: Episcopal, United Presbyterian, United Methodist, and United Church of Christ. Popularly called the Blake-Pike proposals, this initiative led to the formation of COCU—the Consultation on Church Union.

It prompted a long and lively discussion in the entire Christian community; it was alternately praised and damned, depending how one perceived the reality of the ecumenical movement and how an individual or congregation chose to interpret Jesus' great high-priestly prayer in John 17:20-21:

> I do not pray for these only [his disciples], but also for those who believe in me through their word, that they all may be one; even as thou, Father, art in me, and I in

thee, that they also may be in us, so that the world may
believe that thou has sent me.

Followers of Christ, whether they be lay leaders,
seminary theologians, or hospital chaplains, have come
to understand this passage to be essential to Christian
unity. The main demonstration to the world that
Christians are the living representatives of Jesus Christ is
understood most powerfully in their oneness of spirit
and their abiding linkage of cooperation and outreach.
Many would hold that a splintered and fractured body of
believers, divided and subdivided into hundreds of
competing and, at times, combative groupings is an
offense to Jesus Christ and a scandal in the eyes of the
non-Christian world. Many Christians resisted the
Blake-Pike proposals, however, fearing the creation of a
"Super Church" and wary of jeopardizing their historic
theological creeds or liturgical practices. All ecumenical
conversations sooner or later cause waves of crisis
regarding ordination, communion, and sacramental
disagreements.

Below the normal strains and tensions and, at times,
suspicions among various Christian bodies, the Gallup
Poll has uncovered some significant new material that
suggests possible areas of agreement and cooperation
in the coming decade for the churches. This material
was compiled by asking the American public, in
surveys projecting to some 150 million adults, how they
felt—positively or negatively—regarding the convictions and practices of their neighbors in the realm of
organized religion.

Using the Gallup scalometer, the Gallup Organization asked people questions, such as: "How far up the scale or down the scale would you rate Baptists?" A dozen or more religious bodies were listed in such a way as to evoke a response from the general public in regard to their feelings, perceptions, attitudes, and understandings of that particular group.

The compilation of data revealed that Catholics in North America are most positive about their relations with *other* Christian groups. In responding to the question "How far up the scale or how far down the scale would you rate Protestants?" 87 percent of the Catholics interviewed gave a positive rating, with a tiny 2 percent negative rating.

When the Protestants were asked the same question (about themselves) only 82 percent were positive and at least 5 percent expressed negative feelings, indicating at this point that the Catholics are slightly more positive about Protestants than the Protestants are themselves!

When the studies became more specific and asked questions about particular denominations, the Catholic community consistently responded most favorably to their brothers and sisters who belong to other churches. For instance, the seven different religious bodies were asked to scale their feelings up or down, regarding the Lutherans in the United States. The Catholics reflected an 80 percent positive feeling, equal to the sentiments of the Methodists toward the Lutherans and exceeding the positive reactions of both Presbyterians and Baptists. The Catholic response toward Presbyterians and Episcopalians was also more positive than that of Methodists or Baptists regarding those denominations.

Reaching across inter-faith boundaries with positive sentiments toward the Jewish community, the Catholics in America hold the second highest rating along with the Lutherans at 81 percent; the highest rating for this scale belonged to the Episcopalians at 82 percent. Following at lower percentages were the positive responses of the Presbyterians, Methodists, and Baptists. The ecumenical feeling of Roman Catholics in America is a large, moving, generous tide of interest and apparent affection. It is one of the most powerful signs that more and more inter-faith connections and activities can be proposed and adopted. The 1980s can be a time of dramatic advance in church history for Catholic/Protestant relations. Simultaneously Christian/Jewish conversations, leading to cooperative experience, may develop that have never before been attempted or considered.

In fact, one of the clearest signs from this poll of interdenominational and inter-faith feeling is that the potential for cooperation between the major established religious groupings is vast. The possibilities of joint projects, mutual efforts in serving human need, is practically unlimited. Religious structures and historic churches that once were violently opposed to each other, and more than once lethal in their response to one another, now express appreciation, even affection, for one another. It may be that the men and women of the churches in America are way ahead of their leaders. The laity wants this new era of cooperation and amity to find legitimate and prompt expression. It may be that their representatives, the clergy hierarchy involved in talks, are not reflecting the strong currents swelling and surging in their constituencies. Often, designated leaders, particularly those with entrenched power of office or profession, tend to thwart the movement of the people because they fear decline of influence or even loss of office should mergers, organic union, or federations actually take place. Then again, sometimes actual, constitutional, legal merger is not the great priority of the hour and only causes frustration and negative reactions among the participants. The highest urgency is to find the area of *mutual* service and outreach (and mission that by-passes the sticky, organic issue) which permits the joyful and inspiring flow of faith into action with all men and women of goodwill. *That climate now exists.* The movement for spiritual connection is in place. It is only for the present leaders—or their replacements—of the major Christian bodies to recognize this and find the avenues to give it expression.

When Bishop Patrick Kalilombe, W.F., the prominent Christian leader of the Republic of Malawi, visited the United States in 1979, he had an extended and lively interview with the Graymoor community in New York State. At this Catholic ecumenical center of the Atonement Friars, he had the following exchange with Father Daniel Egan:

Father Egan: Do you mean that there are customs and attitudes indigenous to African culture which make the practice of ecumenism easier on the village level than on the bishops' level?

Bishop Kalilombe: Certainly. On the bishops' level, we wait for the Protestants to come to us. The thinking often is this: "We are right and they are wrong. True, history may show that we Roman Catholics have done wrong in the past, but only in minor matters! The Protestants have done most of the wrong." When the people are at Sunday Mass, or when I visit them in their villages, they seem to follow our lead, but only on the surface. When they leave Mass and return to the villages where they express their basic Christian beliefs, they do what we Africans have always done from tribal days. They do what the Spirit of Christ has inspired them to do long before Western missionaries came to Africa. It is present in our very roots, inherent in our very culture, that everyone in the village unites at times of joy and sadness, at a death or marriage, a burial or birth. In contrast to your Western culture, religion is basic to African life. For example, there may be a Hindu prayer, a Moslem reading, a Methodist hymn used at a Roman Catholic funeral. This is basic cultural ecumenism. Some bishop may order such things stopped, but the African way is to smile, say "Yes, bishop," and then go on doing what they have been doing under God's inspiration for many centuries.[1]

[1]Father Daniel Egan, "Interview with Bishop Kalilombe," *Ecumenical Trends*, 8 (September 1979), 127.

Appendix

The following pages present selected data from recent Gallup polls on which this book is based. These are just a tiny sampling of the many questions included in polls conducted in the ongoing search for what Americans are thinking about their religious experience, the world around them, and their own life. The results included here represent the type of raw data on which the authors have based their commentary on religion in America.

First, selected questions from two polls of youth provide data on confidence in the church, the importance of attending church, and belief in God; the importance of religious beliefs; and, to what extent young people believe the law of love and religious beliefs affect daily life. Report A is from a Gallup Associated Press Youth Survey. Reports B and C are from The Survey of Young Adults in Greater Dayton, sponsored by the Miami Valley Young Adult Ministry, Inc.

Charts D and E give the results from two questions asked in a poll on family life conducted for the "Help for Families" seminar sponsored by The Southern Baptist Convention: the first, on the incidence of shared religious experience in the family; and the second, responses to the question, Does religion strengthen family relationships?

Results in displays F and G are from questions asked in a survey of Catholics regarding issues currently facing the Catholic Church and participation in religious activities. This survey of Catholic press readership was done for The Catholic Press Association and funded by The Lilly Endowment, Inc.

In the last three reports, H, I, and J, we see responses from three questions asked in the 1978 study "The Unchurched American" by The Princeton Religion Research Center and The Gallup Organization, Inc., convened and coordinated by the National Council of the Churches of Christ in the U.S.A. The answers recorded here deal with personal values, attitudes toward social change, and attitudes toward organized religion.

The final chart gives an overview of trends in basic religious beliefs and practices in America over the past twenty-five years.

—A—
CONFIDENCE IN CHURCH

Question: "How much confidence do you, yourself, have in the church or organized religion—a great deal, quite a lot, some, or very little?"

	Great deal	Quite a lot	Some	Very little	None	Don't know
TOTAL	25%	31%	31%	11%	1%	1%
Boys						
13–15 years	24	29	33	11	2	1
16–18 years	23	31	36	9	*	1
Girls	25	27	30	14	3	1
13–15 years	27	32	29	11	*	1
16–18 years	28	32	29	9	*	2
	26	32	29	11	1	1

A GOOD CHRISTIAN OR JEW
AND NOT GO TO CHURCH (SYNAGOGUE)?

Question: "Do you think a person can be a good Christian or Jew if he doesn't go to church (synagogue)?"

	Yes	No	Don't know
TOTAL	77%	18%	5%
Boys	75	19	6
13–15 years	72	21	7
16–18 years	78	16	6
Girls	75	21	4
13–15 years	75	21	4
16–18 years	82	15	3

BELIEF IN GOD

Question: "Do you believe in God or a universal spirit?"

	Believe	Don't Believe	Don't know
Teen-agers—Nationwide	95%	3%	2%
Boys	94	4	2
Girls	96	2	2
Both Sexes			
13–15 years	95	3	2
16–18 years	95	3	2
Adults			
18–29 years	92	5	3
30 & over	95	3	2

—B—
IMPORTANCE OF RELIGIOUS BELIEFS

Q. How important to you are your religious beliefs -- very important, fairly important, not too important, or not at all important?

-- YOUNG ADULTS, GREATER DAYTON --

	Very	Fairly	Not Too	Not At All	None	No Opinion
	%	%	%	%	%	%
TOTAL	42	38	13	3	2	2
Men	36	35	19	4	4	2
Women	46	40	9	2	1	2
18-24 years	35	40	17	4	1	3
25-29 years	50	34	10	2	3	1
College	39	37	14	4	4	2
Less than college	44	37	13	2	1	3
Protestants	44	40	11	2	*	3
Catholics	45	41	13	1	-	-
Church members	56	35	7	*	-	2

Religious beliefs:						
Very Important	—	—	—	—	—	—
Not Very Important	—	—	—	—	—	—
Believe in personal God..	55	38	6	—	—	1
Don't believe in personal God	27	38	21	6	5	3
Very happy	48	34	13	4	*	1
Not very happy	36	42	14	3	3	2
Have used drugs	34	34	19	6	5	2
Have not used drugs	48	40	9	1	—	2
Have great deal of confidence in organized religion	64	29	5	—	—	2
Do not have great deal of confidence	21	44	22	6	5	2

*Less than one percent.

POSSIBLE TO PRACTICE LAW OF LOVE?

Q. *One of Christ's main teachings was the idea of love of human kind --
or love of neighbor. As things stand today, how far do you think it's
possible to practice this teaching and still get ahead in the world --
all the way, part of the way, a little of the way, or not at all?*

YOUNG ADULTS, GREATER DAYTON

All of the way 35%

Part of the way   36

A little of the way   13

Not at all   6

Don't know   10

RELIGION AFFECT DAILY LIVING?

2. To what degree do your religious beliefs affect your daily thinking or acting -- a great deal, some, hardly any or not at all?

YOUNG ADULTS, GREATER DAYTON

Great deal	26%
Some	39
Hardly any	14
Not at all	12
No opinion	9
	100%

SHARED RELIGIOUS EXPERIENCE

—D—

Question: "Which, if any, of these have you done with your child or children during the last seven days?"
(Based upon households with children.)

	Said grace at meals	Attended church services	Attended church-related activities	Read Bible together	Talked about God/ religion	Prayed/ meditated	Watched/ listened to religious programs	None of these
NATIONAL	42%	38%	28%	17%	44%	31%	23%	17%
SEX								
Male	38	33	22	15	34	23	19	21
Female	45	43	32	18	51	38	26	14
RACE								
White	42	41	28	17	45	32	21	17
Non-White	43	23	25	18	29	25	33	18
EDUCATION								
College	51	46	34	21	48	39	18	13
High School	38	35	24	14	41	28	24	18
Grade School	35	37	34	22	44	28	31	25
REGION								
East	32	34	23	12	43	25	16	22
Midwest	45	42	29	19	43	34	26	13
South	47	39	30	15	43	29	26	15
West	41	38	28	22	46	40	22	20
AGE								
Total Under 30	29	26	17	8	26	28	17	18
18 - 24 years	21	18	10	8	17	24	18	16

30 - 49 years	51	47	35	22	58	36	27	16
50 & older	36	36	26	14	25	20	18	18
INCOME								
$20,000 & over	52	45	35	16	49	39	22	13
$15,000 - $19,999	39	36	19	13	45	26	18	22
$10,000 - $14,999	39	38	26	22	36	32	26	15
$ 7,000 - $ 9,999	24	41	33	17	45	24	28	22
$ 5,000 - $ 6,999	16	8	10	8	19	15	23	37
$ 3,000 - $ 4,999	30	41	22	9	41	13	22	13
Under $3,000	68	27	41	36	68	54	41	*
RELIGION								
Protestants	49	38	30	19	43	33	27	16
Catholics	33	46	27	14	43	29	18	16
CITY SIZE								
1,000,000 & over	32	36	25	17	40	30	18	22
500,000 - 999,999	38	39	26	19	42	31	14	24
50,000 - 499,999	47	37	28	17	42	28	28	12
2,500 - 49,999	44	48	36	21	44	37	29	7
Under 2,500, Rural	45	39	27	14	48	34	24	18
Religion very important								
when growing up	55	58	59	69	54	58	58	29
Fairly important	31	27	27	19	31	30	29	40
Hardly important at all	10	9	9	8	9	8	8	21
Not at all important	4	6	5	5	7	4	5	8

DOES RELIGION STRENGTHEN FAMILY RELATIONSHIPS?

Question: "To what extent, if at all, has religion in your home strengthened family relationships — a great deal, somewhat, hardly at all, or not at all?" (Based upon households with children.)

	Great deal	Somewhat	Hardly at all	Not at all	No opinion
NATIONAL	45%	35%	10%	8%	2%
SEX					
Male	41	36	10	10	3
Female	48	35	11	6	*
RACE					
White	43	36	11	8	2
Non-White	55	32	6	4	3
EDUCATION					
College	47	33	10	7	3
High School	44	37	11	7	1
Grade School	48	34	4	14	*
REGION					
East	36	41	14	8	1
Midwest	48	33	11	7	1
South	50	34	8	5	3
West	44	35	7	14	*
AGE					
Total Under 30	33	44	10	10	3

	55	26	13	5	1
50 & older	55	26	13	5	1
INCOME					
$20,000 & over	51	32	8	7	2
$15,000 - $19,999	37	37	13	13	*
$10,000 - $14,999	39	42	11	5	3
$ 7,000 - $ 9,999	51	33	11	5	*
$ 5,000 - $ 6,999	29	48	10	11	2
$ 3,000 - $ 4,999	61	17	9	6	7
Under $3,000	73	18	9	*	*
RELIGION					
Protestants	47	37	9	6	1
Catholics	44	34	11	8	3
CITY SIZE					
1,000,000 & over	44	33	10	10	3
500,000 - 999,999	49	23	18	9	1
50,000 - 499,999	39	42	8	9	2
2,500 - 49,999	56	36	6	2	*
Under 2,500, Rural	45	36	11	7	1
Religion very important					
when growing up	66	23	4	5	2
Fairly important	27	52	13	6	2
Hardly important at all	22	31	23	20	4
Not at all important	21	27	12	37	3

* Less than one percent.

OPINIONS ON ISSUES CURRENTLY

FACING THE CATHOLIC CHURCH

Divorced Catholics should be permitted
to re-marry in the Catholic Church 69%

Divorced Catholics should NOT be permitted
to re-marry in the Catholic Church 23

Catholics should be allowed to practice
artificial means of birth control. 73

Catholics should NOT be allowed to practice
artificial means of birth control. 18

The Catholic Church should relax its standards
forbidding all abortions under any circumstances 44

The Catholic Church should NOT relax its standards
forbidding all abortions under any circumstances   47

The Catholic Church should permit the old-style
Latin Mass..64

The Catholic Church should NOT permit the old-style
Latin Mass..26

The Catholic Church should become more ecumenical,
that is, should try to develop closer relations between
Catholics and non-Catholics 84

The Catholic Church should NOT become more ecumenical,
that is, should NOT try to develop closer relations between
Catholics and non-Catholics 7

In general, I approve of the changes in the Catholic Church
since Vatican II 67

In general, I DISapprove of the changes in the Catholic
Church since Vatican II..............................23

NOTE: The "no opinion" figure for each issue has been omitted.

—G—

RELIGIOUS ACTIVITIES IN PAST MONTH

Question: "By any chance have you, yourself, done any of the following within the last 30 days? Just read off the numbers."

	Said Rosary	Meditated	Read Bible	Attended Catholic social function	Gone to confession	Attended meeting of Roman Catholic organization
NATIONAL	36%	32%	23%	21%	18%	10%
SEX						
Male	29	30	19	21	17	10
Female	42	33	27	21	18	9
EDUCATION						
College background	30	45	25	24	16	13
High school	36	27	22	19	17	8
Grade school	50	22	24	20	27	9
REGION						
East	35	30	20	17	16	7
Midwest	33	34	22	28	21	13
South	37	27	24	21	14	10
West	44	37	31	15	17	12
AGE						
18 - 29 years	24	23	17	16	12	6

30 - 49 years	25	37	24	23	14	12
50 & older	22	35	28	22	26	12
MARITAL STATUS						
Married	37	33	25	22	19	11
Single	26	27	14	18	13	8
Divorced/separated	41	34	24	14	15	3
Widowed	55	31	30	22	24	8
RELIGIOUS BELIEFS ARE:						
Very important	48	41	31	27	26	10
Fairly important	26	23	16	16	10	6
Not too/not at all important	10	21	9	7	4	2
Approve of Vatican II changes	37	35	26	23	18	11
Disapprove of changes	43	31	18	19	22	9
Attended church once during last 7 days	43	34	29	26	24	12
Attended twice or more	54	58	35	41	39	24
Did not attend church	23	22	13	8	4	3
Readership of Diocese paper:						
Light	40	40	26	28	20	14
Moderate	50	44	34	32	28	17
Heavy	58	39	36	35	29	18
Readership of national publication:						
Light	40	45	25	32	22	17
Moderate	42	42	29	30	23	16
Heavy	61	49	37	32	28	19

I. GENERAL ATTITUDES

A. Personal Values

Now I would like to read you these statements. Would you tell me after each, whether you strongly agree, moderately agree, are uncertain, moderately disagree or strongly disagree.

	Strongly Agree	Moderately Agree	Uncertain	Moderately Disagree	Strongly Disagree	Don't know/ No answer	
Duty comes before pleasure							
CHURCHED	60%	30%	5%	4%	1%	*	= 100%
UNCHURCHED	48	32	8	8	3	1	= 100%
Commitment to a meaningful career is very important to me							
CHURCHED	56%	27%	8%	4%	4%	1%	= 100%
UNCHURCHED	54	29	8	6	1	2	= 100%
Facing my daily tasks is a source of pleasure and satisfaction							

UNCHURCHED	.31	47	11	8	2	1 = 100%

I have discovered clear-cut goals and a satisfying life purpose

CHURCHED	45%	37%	12%	4%	2%	* = 100%
UNCHURCHED	31	39	19	6	3	2 = 100%

Depending on how much strength and character a person has, he can pretty well control what happens to him

CHURCHED	44%	40%	7%	6%	3%	* = 100%
UNCHURCHED	48	36	6	6	3	1 = 100%

Despite all the newspaper and TV coverage, national and international happenings rarely seem as interesting as things that happen in my own community

CHURCHED	16%	34%	12%	26%	11%	1% = 100%
UNCHURCHED	14	29	13	28	14	2 = 100%

* Less than one percent.

B. Acceptance of Social Change

Here are some social changes which might occur in coming years. (HAND RESPONDENT CARD) Would you welcome these or not welcome them?

More emphasis on self-expression	Welcome	Not Welcome	DK / NA	
CHURCHED	.71%	17%	12%	= 100%
UNCHURCHED	.78	12	10	= 100%

Less emphasis on money				
CHURCHED	.70	20	10	= 100%
UNCHURCHED	.69	23	8	= 100%

More acceptance of sexual freedom				
CHURCHED	.19	72	9	= 100%
UNCHURCHED	.37	52	11	= 100%

More emphasis on technological improvements				
CHURCHED	.75	11	14	= 100%
UNCHURCHED	.75	14	11	= 100%

More emphasis on traditional
family ties

CHURCHED	.94	3	3	= 100%
UNCHURCHED	.87	7	6	= 100%

More respect for authority

CHURCHED	.91	4	5	= 100%
UNCHURCHED	.84	10	6	= 100%

Less emphasis on working hard

CHURCHED	.21	74	5	= 100%
UNCHURCHED	.29	63	8	= 100%

More acceptance of marijuana
usage

CHURCHED	.12	83	5	= 100%
UNCHURCHED	.28	65	7	= 100%

II. ATTITUDES TOWARD ORGANIZED RELIGION

	Strongly Agree	Moderately Agree	Uncertain	Moderately Disagree	Strongly Disagree	Don't know/ No opinion	
Most churches and synagogues today have lost the real spiritual part of religion							
CHURCHED	22%	30%	10%	24%	14%	*	= 100%
UNCHURCHED	30	30	21	14	4	1	= 100%
Most churches and synagogues today are too concerned with organizational as opposed to theological or spiritual issues							
CHURCHED	18%	29%	17%	23%	13%	*	= 100%
UNCHURCHED	26	30	27	11	5	1	= 100%
An individual should arrive at his or her own religious beliefs independent of any churches or synagogues							
CHURCHED	51%	25%	9%	10%	5%	*	= 100%
UNCHURCHED	65	21	7	4	2	1	= 100%

today are not effective in helping
people find meaning in life

CHURCHED 15%	24%	15%	25%	21%	*	=	100%
UNCHURCHED 18	31	22	18	9	2	=	100%

Most churches and synagogues
today are not concerned enough
with social justice

CHURCHED 12%	20%	24%	28%	15%	1%	=	100%
UNCHURCHED 15	24	35	17	8	1	=	100%

Most churches and synagogues
today are not warm or accepting
of outsiders

CHURCHED 10%	18%	15%	30%	27%	*	=	100%
UNCHURCHED 15	22	27	23	12	1	=	100%

The rules about morality preached
by the churches and synagogues
today are too restrictive

CHURCHED 6%	15%	15%	31%	33%	*	=	100%
UNCHURCHED 12	23	30	21	13	1	=	100%

* Less than one percent

TRENDS IN BASIC RELIGIOUS BELIEFS AND PRACTICES OVER LAST QUARTER CENTURY

BELIEFS ABOUT JESUS CHRIST

What do you believe about Jesus Christ – do you think Jesus Christ was God, another religious leader like Muhammad or Buddah, or do you think Jesus Christ never actually lived?

PERCENT SAYING "GOD" OR "SON OF GOD"

1978	████████████████	80 %
1965	███████████████	75 %
1952	████████████████	81 %

PRAYER

Do you ever pray to God?

PERCENT SAYING "YES"

1978	██████████████████	89 %
1965	███████████████████	92 %
1952	███████████████████	92 %

IMPORTANCE OF RELIGION IN PEOPLE'S LIVES

How important would you say religion is in your own life — would you say very important, fairly important, or not very important?

PERCENT SAYING "VERY IMPORTANT"

1978	███████████	53 %
1965	███████████████	70 %
1952	████████████████	75 %

RELIGIOUS TRAINING AS A CHILD

Did you yourself happen to receive any religious training as a child?

PERCENT SAYING "NONE"

1978	████	17 %
1965	██	9 %
1952	█	6 %

Note: The 1952 and 1965 surveys were conducted for the Catholic Digest — the 1952 survey by Ben Gaffin and Associates and the 1965 survey by the Gallup Organization, Inc.